From Rags to Enrichment

From Rags to Enrichment

How I Define Success in Business and in Life

Wayne B. Brown

FIRST EDITION, SEPTEMBER 2024

Published in the United States by WayneWorks, LLC, 2024.

The Library of Congress has cataloged this edition as follows:

Brown, Wayne B., 1961, January 30 -
From Rags to Enrichment: How I Define Success in Business and in Life by Wayne B. Brown −1st U.S. ed.

ISBN: 979-8-9916538-1-7

Book cover and interior design by Doreen Hann
Editing by Cathryn Castle Garcia, C2G2Productions.com

DEDICATION

For Dana, who has enriched my life beyond measure.

"Happiness has no frontiers; it's a state of mind and not a possession, not a set route through life."

~ Robin Lee Graham, *Dove*

ABOUT THE AUTHOR

To learn more about author Wayne Brown, click the QR code.

FOUR BRANDS, ONE FAMILY.

Choose your adventure.
Aggressor.com

AGGRESSOR
ADVENTURES ®

Aggressor Liveaboards

Aggressor River Cruises

AGGRESSOR SIGNATURE LODGES Where Life Happens

AGGRESSOR FLOATING RESORTS at Sea, at Land, at Your Service

Sea of Change Foundation
SeaOfChange.com

SEA OF CHANGE FOUNDATION

TABLE OF CONTENTS

FOREWORD
By Doug McNeese

The first time I met Wayne Brown, we just clicked. I recognized him as someone special, the kind of person who leaves a lasting impression on everyone he meets. Our mutual love of the ocean and scuba is what brought us together, but what sits at the core of our friendship is our shared perspective on what it takes to develop and grow a successful business.

Those who know Wayne might wonder if the first word he spoke as a baby was, "Why?" His curiosity is the driving force that compels him to challenge the status quo. He's always wondering, "How can we do it better; how can we be the best?" Wayne has a keen eye for business, and he has, as he calls it, a highly sensitive "BS detector." He's a straight shooter. Wayne understands that exceptional service is the key to providing a positive customer experience, which in turn, lays the foundation of a profitable business.

Wayne left his family's farm in rural Florida at age 18 to enlist in the U.S. Air Force as a medic. After eight years of decorated military service, he went to work for Taco Bell Corporation, quickly moving from manager to franchise owner. In the span of a few decades, he grew his holdings to include more than 60 Taco Bell locations before selling them in 2006. Not long after, he combined his passion for scuba diving and luxury travel by acquiring the Aggressor and Dancer fleets of liveaboard dive yachts. In 2018, he rebranded the company as Aggressor Adventures, expanding into river cruises and safari lodges, solidifying his position as a leading provider of 5-star luxury adventures worldwide. He also founded Sea of Change, a nonprofit organization dedicated to ocean conservation.

And it appears he's just getting started.

Wayne's adventurous life is making for some good stories. And he is a good storyteller. In this book, he shares his unique and sometimes unconventional perspective on what success really means—and how simple it can be to achieve it for yourself. His stories will no doubt entertain you, but they also might inspire you to drive positive change within your organization, motivate your team, and grow as an effective leader.

But this isn't a formulaic business how-to book. He shares personal anecdotes about his family and friends, challenges some so-called business norms, reveals a few of his owns missteps along the road to success, and identifies the "pet peeves" he regularly deals with as an entrepreneur. Wayne's honest, down-to-earth style of chronicling his personal "from rags to enrichment" experience will probably leave you feeling like you've just spent time gaining valuable wisdom from a trusted friend.

So, buckle up and enjoy a journey into the world of Wayne Brown. Let this book be your guide as you embark on your own thrilling adventures and discover the true meaning of success. The adventure begins now!

PREFACE
What do I want readers to get out of this book?

When I first started out as a manager with Taco Bell corporate, I struggled with interviewing potential new employees and deciding after the interview if they were a good fit or not. Certain individuals were an easy "yes" and others were an obvious "no," but it seemed like most candidates fell someplace in between. Since I was unsure how to decide, I asked Taco Bell HR for reference material on the best interview questions to ask, behaviors to watch for, and any other tips that might help me make solid hiring decisions.

What did I get? Crickets. I found it difficult to believe such a large corporation didn't have these resources, so I started investing in books on interviewing techniques, personnel management, increasing workplace productivity, and more. I did find a lot of useful information, but it would have been nice to have it all in one place instead of having to hunt for it.

I promised myself that one day I would gather up what I'd learned and compile it into a guide for aspiring leaders and entrepreneurs. This book is my attempt to make good on that promise.

As I started writing this book, I thought I was writing a straightforward how-to guide for business leaders. Then it occurred to me that much of what I've learned over the years was influenced by my life, including where I grew up and how I was raised, my time in the military, and my decision to leave the corporate world and strike out on my own as an entrepreneur. I also realized how my wife and family factor into every decision I make. It made me understand that to share what I've learned I'd need to share some of my life story. I'd need to provide some context that I hope will enable you to "see where I'm coming from."

What you'll read here is a very personal account of how I define success, what motivates me to succeed, and why. As much as I wish it was a step-by-step guide to sure-fire success, it's not. Instead, it's a collection of essays I hope will provide insight into how the decisions I've made in both my personal life and my business life have added up to what I call enrichment.

I don't envision you reading this book in one sitting. I hope you'll keep it on your desk and reach for it when you've got a few minutes to spare, and you could use a fresh perspective or maybe some encouragement.

I hope you'll enjoy reading this book. If you come away with one bit of wisdom you can use to your benefit, I'll count that as success.

INTRODUCTION
Living the Dream Versus Making Dreams Come True

Almost everyone that has obtained some level of success is asked about their "What did you want to be?" childhood dreams. I wasn't one of those kids who, early on, had a passion for one career or another. I don't ever remember my parents talking to me about it, although my great aunt once encouraged me to go to medical school. Growing up on a farm about an hour south of Jacksonville, Florida, I'd helped birth cows and tended to injured pets, and I've butchered my share of chickens and other livestock. Instead of being squeamish about blood and guts, I was kind of fascinated.

I can't say I was a good student. In fact, I did just enough to get by and to stay out of trouble with my teachers. School didn't interest me. I was more interested in going to the beach or hanging out with friends than studying.

During my junior year in high school, I took a health class that included volunteering at the local hospital and nursing home. I ended up doing a stint in the imaging lab, which I found extremely interesting. I probably exhausted the technician with question after question. I then transferred to the emergency room, mostly wheeling patients to x-ray. I was fascinated by the chaos of it all. There was so much happening all at once. My time volunteering in the ER led me to think I might be good at something in the medical field.

I knew I didn't have the discipline to take college seriously, so during my senior year in high school I started thinking about joining the military and maybe becoming a medic. A couple friends that were military advised me that if I decided to enlist, to make sure I was assigned to medic school before I signed the enlistment papers. They told me the recruiters would tell me I could decide once I was in basic training and advised me to hold out and have my choice guaranteed. The US Air Force was my preferred branch, so I went to that recruiter first. When I said I wanted to become a medic, he replied just as my friends had warned, saying I could make that choice during basic training. I told him if he could not guarantee I'd be trained as a medic, I would move along to the next military branch recruiter. Suddenly, he was able to produce the paperwork that included assigning me to a medic class following my basic training.

Looking back on it, I could have not picked a better path. I thrived on the structure and order of military life. Within a year, I'd gained the motivation and self-discipline I needed to start taking college courses, military leadership courses and any other advancement programs I could find.

Maybe I wasn't that kid who "just knew" what I wanted to be when I grew up. But I think I've always been that person who, once I decided what I wanted to do, relentlessly pursued the goal.

MAKING IT IN THE MILITARY

After basic training in San Antonio, TX, I transferred to Wichita Falls for an eight-week medic training program. A few weeks before I graduated, I received my first military assignment to the hospital at Kessler Air Force Base in Biloxi, MS. I was barely 18 and out on my own for the first time in my life. At that point I hadn't traveled west of my home state of Florida. The military put me up in barracks and gave me a meal card to use in the dining hall. I had a roof over my head and three meals a day. That felt good. I was excited to start my military career.

My goal was to be assigned to the emergency room. I loved the excitement, never knowing who would walk in the door with an acute illness or injury, or what types of traumas might arrive by ambulance. So, when I met the First Sergeant who was to decide where I'd start work, I might have embellished a little on my past emergency room experience. It worked, because I did get assigned to the ER. When I showed up for my first shift, I learned from several people that, "no one ever got assigned to work the ER without first paying their dues in another part of the hospital." I shrugged it off and just dug into learning everything I could. My "fake it" had worked. Now it was time to "make it." As it turned out, I was well suited for the work, and I really enjoyed it.

Everyone in the ER, from the enlisted to officers, worked as a tight-knit team. We became very close friends. Kessler was a teaching hospital, so we had doctors and dentists completing their rotation with us. They enjoyed the friendly atmosphere and were happy to be included at gatherings on the weekends.

Just one year later, in the fall of 1980, my roommate's girlfriend insisted I should meet Dana, a beautiful young woman who worked as a respiratory therapist at the local civilian hospital. I didn't want our first meeting to be on a blind date, so we agreed to meet while she was on a break at work. Dana mostly worked the night shift, so her break was scheduled quite late. I admit I might have had a drink (or two) to solidify my courage ahead of that first meet-up. Luckily, we hit it off and she agreed to go out with me.

Our first date was simple enough, a dinner and a movie. Soon, we were spending all our time together and by early 1981 I proposed. We were married in June of 1981. I was 20 years old, and Dana was 22. Looking back, dang we were young! At this point, having children was not in the plan. We spent our free time hanging out with other couples, riding my motorcycle along the backroads of Mississippi, and visiting my family in Florida on long weekends.

In the fall of 1982, I received orders to report to Texas in January 1983 for flight medical school, to train as an aeromedical technician. I was assigned to Rhein-Main Air Base, Germany, where I would be working military flights around Europe and Africa. The aircraft were set up as flying ERs, with all the equipment we'd need to handle ill and injured military personnel.

BECOMING A MILITARY FAMILY

We landed in Germany on the first day of Spring, 1983. It felt like the dead of winter. It was sleeting! Having just come from Mississippi, neither Dana or I had winter clothing, so I set off to get my military-issued cold weather gear and then we immediately went to the base exchange to buy warm clothing.

Flying aeromedical evac missions called for some long days, but I enjoyed it. We did have some weekend flights that overnighted in Turkey, and every Friday we returned military members to the USA for treatment that was unavailable in Germany. Those flights returned on Tuesday. It meant many nights away from Dana and our life together, but we understood it was all part of being in the military. I think this is one reason why military families form strong bonds, especially when you are stationed overseas and have no other immediate family or friends nearby. I knew Dana would have the support of our military family while I was away. And I'm happy to report that all these years later we are still in close contact with many of our friends from that time.

In late 1983 we started talking about having a baby. Dana was 23 and back then, age 30 was considered "old" for childbearing. I know that sounds strange now, but it was the norm back then. In May of 1984, our son, Justin, was born at the military hospital in Wiesbaden, Germany. In the middle of the night. Dana and I were thrilled. The nurse handed him to me, instructing me to take my newborn son to the nursery down the hall. I stopped about halfway. He was just so wide-eyed and awake. I marveled at this tiny person, my son. I could not believe I was a father and how incredible it felt. I remember thinking, why hadn't we done this sooner! When I finally arrived at the nursery the nurse checked the time of birth and told me they must have recorded it wrong—seems I'd been standing in the hallway holding Justin, just staring at him, for more than an hour!

Nothing could have prepared me for the deep sense of connection I felt as a father, and how it strengthened our marriage and sense of family. It was a blessing to see our son grow and learn. Our little family was doing great.

And then, tragedy struck. I couldn't write this book without sharing the most powerful heartbreak story I've ever lived through.

_____

TRAGEDY

John and Becky were a perfect couple. Young, in love with each other and devoted to their faith. We became close friends during our time in Germany. John and I flew aerovac together and as couples, we would hang out with them and several other couples almost every weekend.

John and I were part of a crew on a C-141 outfitted as a medical aircraft for the weekly Thursday/Tuesday evacuation flights from Germany to the USA. We landed at Wright Patterson Airforce Base, New Jersey. Rob was also part of the enlisted flight crew. Rob was a single guy whose family is from Connecticut, just a couple hours' drive from Wright Patterson. Once we offloaded the patients, we would be off duty until Monday morning, when we reported in for the return flight. Occasionally, Rob would invite us to spend the weekend at his family's house, which was also close to an amusement park and a shopping mall. It was much nicer than hanging out on base for the weekend.

We were at Rob's when we learned a car bomb had exploded in the Rhein-Main AB headquarters parking lot. My squadron commander contacted me with orders to immediately report back to Wright Patterson and call him when we arrived. While in the car on the drive back we heard a radio announcer report there had been two fatalities from the explosion; one of the dead was a man, one was a woman. John's wife Becky was that woman.

When tragedy strikes, certain details stay with you forever, permanently etched in your memory. Everything from who you are with, to the time of day and the weather outside, to the tiniest details about the room you are in or the clothes you have on. I learned this on August 8, 1985, when holding the phone close to my ear, listening to my commander explain that John's wife Becky had been entering the headquarters building when the bomb went off. I heard him say she was dead.

Next, I heard my commander ask me to deliver this news to John. I had never handled this kind of emotional crisis before. I'm not sure what instinct kicked in, but I knew that if I was the one to tell John, he'd forever associate me with his getting the news of Becky's horrific death. I didn't want that. I asked my commander to be the one to break it to John. He agreed. And he gave me full latitude to make whatever decisions I'd need to make on John's behalf.

Understandably, John was devastated. Becky was only 19. Their life together was just getting started. There was no way he could have imagined losing her like this, to a terrorist attack on a military base. We had a long cry together. Through my shock and sadness over Becky's death, I couldn't help but think of Dana and our baby. My commander had told me they were fine, but I was relieved when I was finally able to call Dana, to hear her voice. I told her I was with John, and that I would stay with him for the next several days. The other crew made plans to return to Germany.

Becky's family had to be notified. Our commander offered to contact her parents, but John, having the strong character I have always known, insisted he would deliver the news. When John phoned them, he did so with amazing composure. I sat near him, quietly weeping. Soon, we boarded a flight to Texas to be with Becky's parents and to help coordinate the return of her body. I helped set up a phone line in her parents' house that allowed them direct access to a military liaison who would assist them. Most of the details were worked out after a few days. Since no firm date had been set for Becky's memorial service, John encouraged me to return to Germany and to Dana and Justin.

Back in Germany, everything felt different. You can't go through something like this and not come out changed from it. A sense of ease, of innocence, was lost. Of course, the Air Force security barriers were beefed up, and ID checks at the base entrance became lengthy and thorough. John was offered an honorable discharge from the Air Force, which he accepted. We stayed in touch for a while, but eventually lost contact. Years later, thanks to cell phones and social media, we reconnected. We had a lot of catching up to do, but in almost no time we were as close as we'd been in Germany. I was happy to learn he eventually remarried and raised two sons. We've visited several times, and we stay in touch with regular calls and texts. Our enduring friendship is a great example of the strength of the bonds you make in the military. They're as strong as family ties, or stronger. You hear the term, "brothers in arms" used a lot, but most folks do not understand the significance. John is a true a brother to me.

———————

I am not sure whether the events of the bombing and Becky's death played a role in my decision to leave the military, or not. Sometimes, things just change. Even when you are on what you believe is the right path, the path doesn't always go where you expected it might.

In the military, there are essentially two ways to get promoted to a higher rank. One way is to work hard, learn new skills, and excel at your job. By doing so, you climb the ladder of success one rung at a time and receive merit-based promotions that come with recognition, increased responsibility and pay raises. Another way to get promoted is by what is known as "time in grade" and "time in service" advancement. In other words, you stand around long enough and eventually you get promoted based on how long you've been enlisted. This system operates on assumptions rather than performance—the military kicks you up the ladder because it figures you "should be" capable based on the time you've been enlisted. Instead of being on the ladder of success that you're expected to climb, you're simply standing on a conveyor belt. One unfortunate result of time in grade/time in service promotions is that some people end up in supervisory positions they're not well-qualified to hold. It's not fair to them and it sure as hell isn't fair to the people who must serve under their command.

After almost seven years in the Air Force, I'd had a few supervisors whose leadership skills left me frustrated. I was at the point in my military career where it was time to take stock. At the end of my current enlistment, I would have eight years in the Air Force. If I re-enlisted for the minimum required four more years, that would put me at 12 years served. I could retire with full benefits after 20 years served, so it was "in for 12/stay for 20" decision time. What this means is, if I stayed for 12 years, it would be almost unthinkable to not stay for 20. At that point I'd be 37 years old—young enough to start a career in the private sector and still have a 20-year military pension banked.

At this critical point of deciding my future with the Air Force, I got on the wrong side of a supervisor who made negative comments on my official review. His comments would effectively block me from future promotions. I wasn't happy about it, so I took it up with my commander, who was an amazing leader I admired. We had a great relationship. When my commander reviewed the notation in my file the first thing he asked was, "Is this a joke?" He knew my work ethic and didn't believe the negative report. Thankfully, he was able to override it. While his intervention brought some relief, the review remained part of my official military record. To remove it, I had to go through a lengthy appeal process, which included a formal review by a tribunal. In the end, and with the continued support of my commander, I succeeded in getting the negative review expunged from my record.

I was enjoying my current assignment, operating medevac flights in Europe. However, the ordeal with the tribunal left me wondering if my future military path might also be rife with similar supervisors, and similar BS. I might end up fighting for my next promotion. I made the decision not to re-enlist. I decided I would rather take the management skills I'd learned in the Air Force and put them to use in the private sector where hopefully, incompetent supervisors were not the norm. I asked to be transferred to the local medical clinic Emergency Room for my last year in the service. I had come from four years of working in the emergency room at Kessler Air Force base in Mississippi and had thoroughly enjoyed my time there. I was hopeful I could be useful to them and again, my commander was extremely supportive and helpful in making this happen.

FINISHING STRONG

My last year could not have been better. It turned out the entire clinic had been failing its annual Inspector General inspections and was due for a re-inspection in a few months. I met with the current ER charge nurse and together we set out to ensure at least our department not only passed inspection, but also shined in the process. She started working on all the administrative areas that they had failed on the last inspection. I took over the operational side. I worked many nights after my shift ended, holding classes for all the ER medics on everything from basic life support to advanced cardiac care. We created mock auto wrecks and emergency health drills almost every week. We would work with the medics on what they did well and what needed improvement. During the mock health emergencies, I peppered them with questions on how they reached a diagnosis, what they might have missed, and what they might do differently in the future to achieve better patient health outcomes.

By the time the IG Inspectors returned for the evaluation, the emergency room was ready! I intended to have a mock auto accident to showcase my medics and their skills to the inspectors. The clinic commander said no way in hell he was going to allow me to do that, as he feared it'd lead to more inspection failures. The ER charge nurse intervened, ensuring him we were more than ready. He reluctantly agreed and the time came for our team to shine. Our drill included several "victims" with multiple injuries, some of whom presented symptoms that could be treated in various ways. During one critically injured patient evaluation and treatment, the inspector quizzed me during my triage and treatment, asking why I was treating the patient a certain way in case it was not the internal injury I suspected, but something else. I quickly responded that the treatment I chose was the best available in the field for either situation. I could see the inspectors nod in agreement. The rest of the treatment and transport drill went well. A month or so later, everyone assembled in the base auditorium to learn the results. It turned out that not only was the emergency room the only department to pass the inspection, but I was singled out and called up on stage, where the IG team presented me with an award for exceptional leadership.

This experience helped bolster my confidence. Looking back, I was certain I'd put my time in the military to good use. I felt grateful for the discipline and leadership skills I'd learned during my eight years in the Air Force. Looking forward, I felt I was ready to succeed in the private sector.

A CORPORATE CAREER

When I traded the military for the corporate world, I figured I'd go to work for a large corporation, climb the corporate ladder and I'd be on the road to success. I returned to Jacksonville and interviewed with Pepsico, which at the time also owned Taco Bell, Pizza Hut and KFC. They hired me to fill a store management position. I was certain I could excel within Taco Bell and sure enough, within a year of starting at Taco Bell I was city manager.

I was cruising along just fine in my career, but it wasn't long before I discovered the corporate world is not immune to the type of bureaucratic BS I experienced in the military. One day, I received a call from the area vice president's administrative assistant, insisting I complete an inventory report accounting for all the crew uniforms at every Taco Bell store I managed. I asked when they needed it and she said, "Right away." Now, I worked hard to keep all my store managers focused on customer service. I could not fathom who decided that a uniform inventory report was an urgent matter requiring my immediate attention. I told the admin there was no way I could get all my managers on the phone, have them conduct a physical inventory and then get back to me in the same day. Remember, this was before every business had a computer and inventory tracking software. Once again, the admin insisted it was urgent. So, I called back an hour later and started reciting various unform counts from each store. When I finished, she said, "Wayne, you made all these numbers up, didn't you?" I replied, "Absolutely. You have what you asked for. I'm not wasting any more of my time, or my managers' time, on this."

I didn't hear anything more about the inventory report until a week or so later. That's when a typed, signed letter from the area VP arrived in the mail. She really laid into me, citing my behavior as unprofessional, and warning that such conduct would not be tolerated again. So, I hand wrote a reply on the bottom of her letter, outlining where she had failed as a leader. I mailed it right back to her. At this point, I had been with Taco Bell for two years. And I was doing a good job.

Let me give you some side notes here. Jacksonville was a franchisee training city. Any new franchisees from the eastern half of the country were required to spend several weeks in one of the stores I managed, learning the basics. I always stopped by several times to check in with them and became friends with a lot of them. I asked a lot of questions about their business backgrounds, why they were interested in franchising, and various business questions on finance, etc.

Back to the situation with my area VP. Our region held quarterly meetings to review financials and operations, which usually lasted two or three days. At the end of the last day of meetings, she called me into her office and pulled out the letter I had mailed her weeks earlier. "I'd like you to explain this to me," she said. I immediately thought, here we go again, just like in the Air Force. If she doesn't get it, I'm done. I took a deep breath and replied, "Rather than explain it, I think it'd be best for me to give you my two-week notice. It's time for me to move on." I don't think this was the response she expected. She tried to talk me out of resigning, but if the bureaucracy of corporate world was proving to be as frustrating as the military, maybe it was time for me to strike out on my own. It was time for me to try working for myself.

FROM ZERO TO 60 TO ZERO

Around that time, one of the franchisees-in-training approached me. He explained that he was building one store in Florida and wanted to expand to multiple stores. Taco Bell would not allow him to fast-track his expansion plan unless he had a full-time operations manager. He offered me the opportunity to build a successful franchise operation with unlimited autonomy. . The timing was perfect. We quickly cut a deal and bought the two stores. That was in 1989. We built two more stores together before tragedy struck. He was a passionate aviator and stunt pilot. Sadly he was killed in a plane crash. After his death, I convinced Taco Bell to let me buy the franchise. I continued to grow my franchise businesses and by early 2006, I had 60 stores in the southeast.

That same year I was approached by a private equity firm that wanted to come into the Taco Bell business with a bang. They weren't interested in starting out small. When they made me an offer to buy all my franchise holdings, I had to give it some serious thought. Long story short, I sold to them in November of 2006.

Was cashing out my definition of success? Honestly, no. This might surprise some people, but no. Building a business that succeeded because of its high standards for customer service—that was what I call success.

Was it "overnight" success? No. I made consistent business wins that accrued over time. Happy customers became repeat customers. It's what helped me grow my business and expand my holdings to 60 Taco Bell locations. Of course, selling the business for a profit was certainly a nice bonus prize, but delivering exceptional customer service is what got me there. It became part of me, and it remains the driving force behind everything I do.

TAKING SCUBA DIVING FROM PASTIME TO PROFESSION

Odds are good that you picked this book up because you know me from my business, Aggressor Adventures, rather than my having once been "the Taco Bell guy." Here's how that happened.

When my son Justin was 15, I realized that once he turned 16 and got his driver's license, I might not see much of him. I knew I needed to make good use of the next year, or we'd miss out on a precious opportunity to spend time together.

I noticed a scuba diving shop located along my daily commute, so I stopped in and asked about lessons. I wondered if scuba diving might be something we'd enjoy together. It turns out, we both loved it.

One of the great things about scuba diving is that the ocean levels the playing field. Scuba diving is the same for everyone in terms of the theory that needs to be learned and the skills that must be mastered. It didn't matter that he was a teenager, and I was his dad. We were learning scuba diving as equals instead of as father and son. Divers are taught to be self-reliant, while at the same time relying on a buddy. As divers, we operated as a buddy team.

That was in 1999 and we've obviously been diving ever since. Not long after my son and I got certified, my daughter Ashley was old enough to get certified and she joined us. Diving became a family activity we could enjoy together. My wife Dana didn't take to scuba the way the kids and I did, but she was fully supportive of our new passion for diving.

We started out doing weekend trips organized by our local dive shop to places like West Palm Beach, Florida. Those were land-based boat charters, which typically depart in the morning for two dives, and then return in the afternoon. Next, we visited popular diving destinations like Cozumel and Grand Cayman. The resorts' dive shops offered day-long boat trips, but we were still only making two or three dives each day. It wasn't long before we tried our first liveaboard, which was a 65-foot sailboat that cruised from Miami to the Bahamas. The goal was to dive, dive, dive. It was fun getting in as many as five dives a day, but the accommodations were far from luxurious. It was like camping at sea. The boat had two big bunkrooms and two bathrooms for 22 divers.

I had heard from other divers that the Galapagos Islands were considered the pinnacle of adventurous scuba diving. Large schools of hammerhead sharks, whale sharks, eagle rays, and tons of fish life were the norm. Intrigued, my daughter and I and four friends booked a weeklong trip onboard the *Galapagos Aggressor* in 2005. This was my first time experiencing the highest level of customer service in the diving industry. Instead of camping at sea, we enjoyed the luxuries of a spacious, well-appointed yacht, with private ensuite cabins, gourmet meals, and a friendly, professional staff. It was an amazing experience as a customer. I decided it was the only way I wanted to go diving ever again!

In 2006 we booked a trip on the *Belize Aggressor*, and I was hooked. I asked who owned the company, thinking I would love to sit down and chat with them about how they got to this level of success in business. I learned the company's founder, Paul Haines, had passed away. After a bit more investigating, I found out the family was interested in selling the Aggressor Fleet business. Having just sold my Taco Bell franchises, I guess you could say the timing was perfect.

And the rest is history. What started as a family pastime was turning into a new business passion. I edited my definition of success as delivering 5-star service to global travelers. I was all over that challenge! In April of 2007 I became the new owner of Aggressor Fleet.

ON ENTREPRENEURSHIP

Don't just accept things the way they are. Make them the way you want them to be.

THE ECLECTIC ENTREPRENEUR

My first year of military service in Germany went well and I was steadily moving up in position within our squadron. Flight evaluator was the highest position you could attain in that squadron. It's an important job, because in addition to training crew in various positions, the job also entails evaluating them for certification as flight techs.

The next time the flight evaluator position became available, my commander, who I respected and was my advocate at the squadron, suggested I apply. Candidates for this position must appear before a review board for an interview. Since my commander, a colonel, had already given me the nod, the interview was just a formality. Thing is, he got called to the Pentagon on the day of my review, so one of the other officers was called in to replace him. During the interview, instead of asking me about various aspects of the flight evaluator position, this guy asks me, "What does 'eclectic' mean?" The question threw me. I wasn't expecting a vocabulary quiz. I replied, "I'm sorry sir, I don't know what that means." Just like that, he killed my promotion to flight evaluator. Over the definition of a word.

When the colonel returned, he was furious. Unfortunately, there was nothing he could do about it.

When I realized I'd been passed over for promotion to flight commander, I was furious, too. And frustrated. I headed straight for the base library, found a dictionary, and looked up "eclectic." What was so frustrating was, after I read the definition, I realized of course I knew the definition. I mean, "eclectic"—which as an adjective is defined as, "to use a method or approach that is composed of elements drawn from various sources"—is a leadership style I practiced every day. When you're in the military and supervising members of a squadron, practicing eclectic leadership is the way to get things done. Some people need a lot of direction. Some people hardly need any. Working in the emergency room, there were times when it seemed everyone needed immediate direction if we were going to succeed at saving a person's life. Maybe I didn't know the definition of the word "eclectic" that day, but I certainly lived it. Every day.

I didn't get promoted, but I learned an important lesson, one that has stayed with me all my life. I learned that words matter. Literally and figuratively. I made it a point to keep a dictionary handy, and to beef up my vocabulary. I turned my anger and disappointment into curiosity and a commitment to always continue learning. I think this lesson served as a major factor in my success in the corporate world and as an entrepreneur.

EARLY EFFORTS

I suppose I've always had an entrepreneurial streak. My earliest memories of working for pay was polishing my father's cowboy boots for a quarter and washing his 18-wheeler Mac truck for a dollar. When I was six years old, he took a break from long-haul trucking and opened a franchise gas station. We lived just down the street from the elementary school, so my older brothers and I walked to school and home every day. The gas station was about a mile away and we'd walk there from school every afternoon. We all had chores at the station. My brothers pumped gas, washed windshields and checked the oil. My job was to greet customers and give out free bubble gum to any cars that came through with children. We would do this on weekdays until closing and then all day on Saturday and Sunday. After a while my father decided to return to trucking, and we moved to a very small farming community about two hours south. When I say small, we had a gas station and grocery store. They were the same place.

Our farm started out with a small garden and a couple of cows. Before long, we had pigs, goats, chickens, turkey and horses. Just like at the gas station, we all had chores. We'd pitch in every morning to feed and water the animals before the school bus came. We repeated the chores again after we got home from school. I never remembered anyone complaining or it being a burden. It was part of ensuring we had food on the table, but we still had plenty of "play" time to hunt the local woods and fish in the ponds.

Our house was several miles from the nearest convenience store, so when I was 12, I decided I could put an old refrigerator/freezer in the barn to use. I stocked it with sodas, candy bars and popsicles. I painted a piece of plywood with prices and nailed it to a fencepost at the entrance of our driveway. There were only about a dozen families in this farming community, but most of them had children and I had high hopes of making a profit of at least a few dollars a day. Unfortunately, I didn't end up saving any money because I helped myself to sodas and candy. I ate and drank all my profits.

This proved to be a good lesson once I became a Taco Bell franchisee. In the early days I took home the smallest salary we could live on, and never pilfered inventory or took any "bonuses" from the cash registers.

EXPERIMENTING

My next foray into entrepreneurship came at age 14, when I tried door-to-door sales, selling shoes from a catalog. I wore my own shoes out, walking to every farmhouse. I ultimately sold one pair. It was to an elderly couple (at least they seemed old back then). When I reflect on that one sale, I'm certain they weren't wowed by my expert sales skills; they were just kind enough to help a kid out.

I tried getting the local feed store owner to hire me to help unload trucks, but he always politely declined. Looking at me, he probably figured that a scrawny young kid couldn't lift one bag let alone unload a hundred.

The following year, I went to the lone restaurant in town, The Pit BBQ. I don't know if the owner believed in me, or took pity on me, but he gave me a chance. It was a small restaurant, so I was a one-man band, cooking, cleaning, washing dishes, helping bus tables and occasionally taking orders.

After a few months I asked the owner (who also owned the small IGA grocery store, the only one in town) if I could create a Sunday Special meal to offer our customers something different. He gave me the green light, probably figuring no harm could come of it, since Sundays were usually slow, with just me and one waitress working. I decided a meatloaf would be easy enough, so I picked up the ingredients from the IGA and made one casserole dish-sized meatloaf. It sold out before the end of lunch and our customers loved it. So, I guess I could say my first big business success was that meatloaf!

I kept working at The Pit BBQ and grinding out Sunday Specials until my junior year of high school. I left to work at a steakhouse that paid more money and allowed me some weekends off.

I'm grateful that the owner took a chance on me and agreed to let me try new things. During that time, I learned about initiative, and how good it felt to be able to be creative at work. I try to keep that in mind when my employees want to propose new ideas.

DEFINING ENTREPRENEURSHIP

What is an entrepreneur, really? If you search the Internet you'll find all sorts of definitions, but basically, an entrepreneur is anyone who sets up, manages, and scales a business.

What does it take to be an entrepreneur? I didn't attend Harvard Business School, but when I set out to write this book, I visited their website to learn what they had to say about entrepreneurship. They have an online course titled Entrepreneurship Essentials. In it, Harvard Business School identifies 10 characteristics of successful entrepreneurs. They are curiosity, willingness to experiment, adaptability, decisiveness, self-awareness, risk tolerance, comfort with failure, persistence, innovative thinking, and long-term focus. I can identify with all these traits, some more strongly than others.

For the purposes of this book, I've sorted my stories into the following categories: Focus and Discipline, Initiative and Leadership Style, Vision and Strategy, Attitude and Adaptability, and Truthfulness and Integrity. I've also included a short section on Bullshit. Because there's a lot of it out there and it's important that you detect it before you step in it. The final section, What Matters Most, includes life lessons I've learned thanks to my family and friends, and the people I've worked with along the way.

A lot of research has been done around the question, "Are entrepreneurs born or made?" Maybe some people are naturals at it. Maybe some people learn it along the way. Maybe it's a bit of both. I'm not here to answer that question for you, but whether you consider yourself an entrepreneur or not, I hope these stories will help you define what success means for you, and what you want your own path to enrichment to look like.

FOCUS & DISCIPLINE

You can't succeed on passion alone. You must be focused and disciplined.

MAKE SURE YOU ARE READY

I pushed off the sandy creek bottom and clawed for the surface, but I only managed to get my eyes above the water line. I couldn't stay afloat long enough to take a breath, but I remember I could see my mother sitting on a beach chair, looking out at the water. Down I went again. I wondered; did she see me? I was eight years old, and I was drowning. I was so near the floating platform at Middleburg Beach, but it was just out of reach. It was quiet under the water. I could feel myself growing tired. I was out of air. I kicked upward once more. I reached the surface but was still unable to take a much-needed breath. This time, she saw me. My mom jumped from her beach chair, pointing and yelling to my brother, who was on the platform. He dove in and pulled me out of the water and onto the platform. I laid on my back, squinting at the sun and taking in big gulps of air. I remember how great it felt to breathe. And how happy I was to be alive.

That experience scared the hell out of me—and my mom and brother, too—but it didn't make me afraid of the water. In fact, it taught me an important lesson that has served me throughout my life.

Eventually, I did learn to swim. A lot of kids learn the basics of how to swim by the time they're eight years old, but not me. I had started swimming lessons at the local YMCA when I was six or seven, but then we moved from Jacksonville, Florida to the small rural town of Middleburg, about an hour south. It was mostly farmland. There wasn't a pool anywhere nearby, so I hadn't learned to swim. When I was 12, I stayed the summer with family in South Carolina and their community had a swimming pool. I bought a pair of fins, mask and snorkel and I spent hours each day, finning back and forth across that pool. Eventually, I was able to swim without them. By the end of the summer, I was comfortable in the water and was a pretty good swimmer. I could swim to the bottom of the deep end, push off the bottom, and return to the surface for a breath, no problem.

I've often thought about that day at Middleburg Beach. The day I was in over my head and couldn't come up for air. It was not on the ocean but on Black Creek. A local businessman owned the property next to the bridge that crossed a wide section of Black Creek. He hauled in some sand and opened a water park he called Middleburg Beach. It was a popular spot for local families to sunbathe and swim—despite that it was also a popular spot for alligators to sunbathe and swim!

One of the main attractions of Middleburg Beach was that floating platform. You could wade out from shore, climb onto the platform and jump off. All the kids loved doing it. What my eight-year-old self didn't know way back then is that the anchor ropes that tethered the platform in place had a lot of slack in them. When I climbed onto the platform, it was in shallow water. I hadn't noticed it floating out from the shallows into deeper water. I was so excited to jump that I didn't notice I was jumping into the deep.

I have used my childhood near-drowning experience as a metaphor, as a gauge of readiness, ever since. A lot of business start-ups operate with a "leap first, then look" mindset—as if passion alone can substitute for proficiency. I'm sure you've heard it put a lot of different ways, including the classic, "No guts, no glory." Passion is an important component of success. And so is risk-assessment. Whenever a new opportunity comes along, I ask myself, "Do I have the skills I need to be successful in this new opportunity?" Before I proceed, I want to make sure I understand what I'm getting into, what the risks are, and what I'll need to learn so I don't fail—and so I eventually succeed. I much prefer to "look first, then leap."

Entrepreneurs are an interesting breed. We love challenges. And we take risks. We love to push the boundaries of our knowledge and skills. But at the same time, we must maintain focus. We must be careful not to jump in too deep in our business deals. Otherwise, we literally risk getting in over our heads. And we could drown.

MAKING IT WORK

My mom was barely five feet tall, but she didn't let her petite frame stop her from doing whatever she wanted or needed to do. She worked at a bank for a while, and she drove a school bus for several years.

When I was a young teenager, she joined my father in his work as a long-haul trucker. They hauled US Mail from Jacksonville to New York City three times a week. Since my mom was too short for her feet to reach the truck floor, my dad made a set of wooden blocks that he'd strap onto the clutch, brake and throttle pedals so she could reach them. This way she could take her turn driving the 18-wheeler, no problem. Working as a team enabled them to cover the miles without stopping much; one drove while the other slept. They worked this gig together for many years.

I showed an interest in cooking at an early age, so I learned a few basic recipes I could cook for myself and my siblings. Our parents expected us to have the self-discipline to behave ourselves and look out for each other while they were on the road. We each did our part as a family to make it work. Looking back, I don't remember it being a hardship.

Back then, long-distance phone calls were expensive, so my mom had a way to check on me in the mornings to make sure I was up and getting ready for school. On the school day mornings when my parents were on the road, the phone would ring. The voice on the other end of the line would be a long-distance operator asking if I would accept the charges. I knew it was my mom checking in from the road even though she always gave the operator a made-up name, just for fun. I knew to decline the charges. She knew I was up and getting ready for school. At least during my early teen years, there was a good chance I was getting ready for school. Once I started driving, I might just have easily ended up at the beach.

EARN YOUR PLACE

As a teenager, my job at The Pit BBQ helped me feel confident that if I worked hard, showed initiative and hustled a bit, I would certainly advance. I applied this work ethic at the local steakhouse, where I started as a dishwasher, and it wasn't long until I advanced to Lead Cook. This promotion was a big deal, as the grill is the heart of any steakhouse.

One very busy Friday evening, I was cranking out steaks as fast as I could—hot off the grill and onto the plates. Because I was rushing, I wasn't paying attention to the plating, making sure the meals looked attractive as they left the kitchen. The steakhouse owner was working the pass and he noticed. When he asked me to take the orders back and properly plate them according to his restaurant's high standards—he insisted a meal must be well-prepared, well-plated, and served with a smile—I responded with something like, "If you don't like the way the plates look, you'll need to re-plate them yourself. I'm busy grilling so we can keep the orders moving."

He did re-plate them. And he did it without saying another word to me.

I came in to work the next day to discover my name was crossed off the schedule. I had been fired. Just like that. I was stunned. I stood there, staring at the page thumbtacked to a bulletin board, at the thick lines drawn with permanent marker through my name. I was so disappointed in myself. I had considered myself such a high achiever—such a valuable employee. I'd never imagined I might get fired.

It stung, but it taught me a valuable lesson. No one is irreplaceable. It doesn't matter how high up in the company you've climbed, or how important your job is. Confident is good. Cocky will cause you trouble. And I'd gotten cocky in my role as Lead Cook.

The lesson here? You must earn your place, and you must continue to earn your place every day. Also, you must stay focused on what's most important about the job you've been hired to do. And if you don't? Well, like 17-year-old me, you might show up to work one day and find you no longer have a job.

SUCCESS IS A FORMULA, NOT A SECRET

I am often asked to share the secret of my success. Bookstores and libraries are full of books on this topic. And here I am, adding another book to the shelf. My book contains a couple hundred pages of essays about entrepreneurship and what it takes to succeed in business and in life, but the fact is, there's no secret to success. There's a simple formula:

A great idea + a relentless work ethic + a little luck = success

There are countless ways to put this formula into practice, but you'll need these three key ingredients. When people ask me for advice, I always start by asking them to tell me about their business idea. Every good business starts with a great idea. Next, I ask who the customer will be. Just because you have what you think is a great idea, it won't work unless there is a market for it. Your idea must be great enough that people will pay money for whatever you've got. The line, "If you build it, they will come" only works in movies. There's got to be a reason why people will show up to buy what you're selling. And to attain lasting success, you'll likely need to do it better or faster or cheaper than the competition.

Let's say your idea has merit and a potential market to be worth the effort, my next question is always, are you willing to do what it takes? Do you have the drive and determination? I am not talking about a few hours a week after your current job or on weekends. I am talking about focusing every hour of every day on making it work.

Even if your idea makes it and you are successful, you can't expect to slack off. The workload just gets heavier. Now you not only have to deliver that idea to customers but work on improving your idea to stay relevant.

Let's go the opposite direction and imagine that even though you have a great idea and you put in the time to make it work, it never takes off. Winston Churchill described perseverance as, "Stumbling from failure to failure with no loss of enthusiasm." Eventually, things turn in your favor. I try hundreds of ideas in my businesses every year. Many of them don't end up creating value for my customers. I do know though that I will learn something from everything I try. It never discourages me. In fact, it's just the opposite. After I examine and process what didn't work, I get excited to try again.

TAKING NOTE

Someone once asked me, "How do you know if you're ready to take on a new business challenge?" My answer is, "I am always ready."

Think about this in terms of taking advantage of every opportunity. I never had a supervisor tell me that there was an opportunity for me to advance, but I just wasn't ready. I think this might be due in part because I have always looked for ways to up my game.

In the Preface of this book, I confided that in my first job as a Taco Bell manager, I wasn't very good at interviewing potential Taco Bell employees because I'd never done it before. There's always a first time for everything, but I wasn't satisfied to just keep fumbling at it. I studied interview techniques, practiced and got better at it. Before long I was confident as an interviewer. This helped me hire the right employees for the job, which in turn, made everything better at work.

This is a fundamental difference in those who achieve success and those who don't. They keep learning. The best thing you can do is be honest about your skills, including what you do well and what you struggle with. Make a list of what you need to work on. The worst thing you can do is say, "Well I suck at that, so I'm not doing it." Instead, improve. There are so many online resources available these days that you can fill a knowledge gap very easily.

One common trait among successful people is that they are often prolific note-takers. My brain has always been on fire with ideas. If I don't record them, I risk losing them, so I keep a notepad and pen handy. Multiple studies have revealed numerous benefits of writing notes by hand. In fact, the February 2024 issue of *Scientific American* contains an article about a study that monitored brain activity in students and found that taking notes by hand produced higher levels of electrical activity across a wide range of interconnected brain regions responsible for movement, vision, sensory processing, and memory. Of course, these days I store notes on my digital devices, but I still write a lot of notes by hand before I transfer them to my phone or computer later. And I keep all my notes, because you never know when the timing might be right to develop an idea.

Here's an example. Ever since my early days of owning Aggressor Fleet, I wanted to create an amazing theme song and video that captured the essence of what we're about. From time to time, I scribbled down some ideas for song lyrics. Ten years passed. Then one day a customer, and now a close friend, on one of our adventures, Jon Michaels, mentioned he was a singer/songwriter. I told him about my idea of having a theme song for Aggressor Adventures. A few weeks later, he sent me a recording of him singing what eventually became the final version. So, take good notes and never give up on your ideas. A good idea will likely pass the test of time. This one took 10 years!

TWEAKING THE FRANCHISE MODEL

People have asked me how a guy who succeeded at owning Taco Bell restaurants figured he'd succeed at floating dive resorts. It's simple, really. In the restaurant and resort industries, the name of the game is customer satisfaction. The way to win the game is to consistently provide the highest possible level of customer service—to make people happy. It doesn't matter if the business serves food or scuba diving adventures, the goal is the same.

The Aggressor business model is not quite a franchise model but more of a license model. I know the franchise world like the back of my hand, so applying my expertise to running Aggressor Fleet wasn't that big a stretch. I am the Licensor in this case. Each destination is locally owned by a Licensee who agrees to operate their dive yacht according to Aggressor Fleet standards.

When I purchased the company, I also purchased three yachts/destinations that were available for sale. One yacht was licensed to operate in Belize, another in the Cayman Islands, and the third in the Turks and Caicos Islands. I knew that owning what the licensees owned would help me intimately understand the business. It would also give the licensees confidence that as "one of them" I understood the business from their perspective. During the first three years of owning Aggressor Fleet, I traveled my butt off, visiting every destination. I spent valuable time with the licensees, learning the local culture, the ways in which that destination's government operated and how it would affect their business operations, and what other challenges they faced. I also wanted to know what they discovered had worked in the past and—just as importantly—what had failed, and why, so we didn't keep repeating any mistakes. A franchise is ultimately a partnership agreement, a relationship. If I was to gain their confidence, they had to know I was fully committed to our mutual success. The only way to gain that confidence is to put in the time.

While I was focusing on the operations side of the business, I also was refining the marketing and advertising. If we were going to present ourselves as the world leader in the adventure business, there would be no more small magazine ads. Only full-page or even two-page spreads, with a new, branded message each month. You have probably noticed companies that create an ad that runs every month, without any changes. They might consider it branding, repeating the same advertising message, but to me it looks like nothing new is happening. I wanted to convey a new and exciting message every month with ads that really stood out and enticed customers to join us.

ASKING IMPORTANT QUESTIONS

Another big challenge I had to undertake early on was updating the fleet-wide SOPs (Standard Operating Procedures). The Haines' team had an SOP manual each licensee was meant to follow, but it needed a comprehensive overhaul.

A task like this one requires curiosity, patience, and meticulous attention to detail. Before a practice becomes "standard practice" it's important to ask a lot of "whys." It's about questioning everything. And I mean everything.

The first questions are, "What are we doing?" and "Why are we doing it?" For Aggressor Fleet, the goal is to provide scuba diving and adventure travel that offers the highest possible level of customer satisfaction. As always, happy customers are our goal.

Next, we ask the "how" question, which is "How will we accomplish our goal?" Before a practice is added to the Standard Operating Procedures manual, it must be "boxed in." The four sides of the "SOP box" represent the following criteria: it must ensure the safety of guests, crew and physical assets; it must streamline operations for maximum efficiency/productivity; it must ensure the greatest level of comfort and enjoyment for guests and crew; and it must deliver the highest possible return on investment for the licensees.

I have a very large conference table in my boardroom that served as the perfect staging area for this project. I started with a physical copy of the original Aggressor SOP manual. It was a thick book with what seemed like hundreds of pages held together in a three-ring binder. I started by separating the current SOPs into sections based on the categories of operations. Next, I spent time meticulously editing, rewriting and updating procedures, making sure each fit in the "box." This is when owning three of the yachts in our fleet, combined with my nearly nonstop travel to visit all our destinations really came in handy. I had learned the operations side of the business well enough to draft a comprehensive set of SOPs.

Once I was done with the bulk of the work, I sent draft copies to key Aggressor Fleet team members for their input. They were instructed not to "reinvent the wheel," but rather to carefully read the procedures and help refine them while keeping the original goals in mind. We tweaked a few procedures until we were satisfied with the final version.

As a side note, if you look on the Internet, you'll find companies advertising "instant" SOPs. Log in, download a template and fill in a few blanks and you're done. I can't believe companies like this exist—or that business owners and managers think a boilerplate SOP manual will help them achieve success.

You must know what business you're in. I think it's important to identify this as a key area where leaders can fail. If a product or business goes from idea to implementation without asking important "what, why and how" questions, it could be doomed from the start. Or it could, over time, be poorly managed to the extent that the business completely loses sight of its original goal. Sometimes managers and employees are "busy" working, but they're not busy doing the important work of ensuring customer satisfaction. I call it Goal Blindness. I saw it in the military, and I saw it early in my career with Taco Bell corporate.

THERE'S NOTHING BORING ABOUT PAYING ATTENTION

It was a long process, but once the Aggressor Fleet SOPs had been fully updated, the next step was to ensure the new procedures were implemented fleet wide. We also put in place measures to make certain that our high standards for customer satisfaction and safety were met. And we implemented a system for examining and updating future SOPs rather than waiting until the procedures manual needed a complete overhaul. I feel that in any company, the SOP should be considered a living document. When new technology or some other factor allows us to change and improve the way we handle a particular procedure, it calls for an update to the SOP.

This might seem like boring work. Obviously, traveling to all the destinations, meeting the yacht owners and crew, and doing a lot of diving was fun. But so was assembling stacks of paper on a conference table. It's one of the most exciting parts of the job. Why? Because when you pay attention to how your business operates, you pay attention to your success. And future growth.

When I purchased Aggressor, the company focused exclusively liveaboard scuba diving yachts. We had eight destinations. Of course, I wanted to open liveaboards in more destinations, but I also knew that to grow the business, I had to expand outside of that niche. I created a River Cruise brand and a Safari Lodge brand using the 5-star model of the liveaboards. Our river cruises take place on smaller vessels perfect for 18 to 20 guests. We keep similar numbers at our lodges, too. This allows our staff of highly trained guides plenty of opportunity to interact with our guests. No walking in a large crowd wearing a headset or trying to hear a guide who is so far ahead you can't even see them. It's all about delivering personalized service intended to ensure the highest guest satisfaction.

Today, I have open or under construction 40 destinations and many more in the initial planning stages. In fact, I have grown the brand to the extent that Ministries of Tourism in countries like India and Saudi Arabia have reached out to me, inviting my company to be the first liveaboard scuba diving brand in their expanding tourism sector. I am also launching another brand called Aggressor Floating Resorts. Why limit yourself to a hotel room. Why not have a yacht for the week? Each evening, we list out the options for you. Tomorrow, you want to go desert four-wheeling, parasailing, shopping, hang out at the local resort pool, snorkel, scuba dive, beach comb or numerous others? Evening champagne cruises on 'your' yacht? Done. There are so many places this will work around the world; it has the potential to be as big as any of my other brands.

FROM SHAKE-UP TO SHAKEDOWN

One of my lead bookkeepers who was responsible for handling international wire transfers to all our destinations around the world abruptly left the company. Her husband was offered a job in a different city on short notice, and she was unable to remain to train her successor, so I stepped in to train her replacement. I wasn't thrilled about the timing of the transition, as it disrupted my schedule. But this disruption turned out to be a good thing, because my spending time handling the wire transfers led me to discover a kink in our system.

While going through the process of figuring out what funds are due to each destination, it seems our bookkeepers had been exporting information from our reservation system and manually entering it into a new spreadsheet. This presented a two-fold problem; first, it was time consuming and second, it was tedious work, with potential for data-entry errors to be made.

I took the problem to our IT department and showed them the format we had to use to figure out the transfer amount, considering all sorts of variables including commissions, discount vouchers and more. I said, "Here's what needs to come out of the reservation system and flow into the accounting system." In two days' time, our lead IT expert was ready to demo a solution. In a couple keystrokes, all the necessary data from the reservation appeared precisely where it needed to be in the accounting system. A task that had taken 30 to 45 minutes per transaction was now being completed in less than five seconds! This integration solution was huge, representing a savings of about 30 data-entry hours per week, maybe more. Plus, automation eliminated the risk of errors that can occur when an employee spends hours each day toggling back and forth from one spreadsheet to another. And it freed up employee time to devote to more productive work. It was a win, win, win!

This is a prime example of disruption as a positive force. Innovations come from disruption. When it came to training a new bookkeeper, I could have made excuses, saying, "I don't have time for this. I can't afford to sit with a new employee for several hours at a stretch, teaching the basics." But my doing so ultimately led to a huge productivity increase. It also prompted me to look deeper into other aspects of our accounting and reservations systems, to envision ways to fully integrate all the data the business needed, in every step of our operation. I got really excited about this project.

As I dug deeper, I discovered that our voucher system was another area that needed improvement. We came out of the pandemic with thousands of vouchers we issued for postponed/rescheduled trips. Our guests didn't want to cancel their vacations but due to government-imposed travel restrictions, we were forced to suspend operations. Rather than refund their payment, we issued vouchers to be applied to future travel. The voucher system was complicated by the fact that during the pandemic, some destinations had early false starts, opening and closing a few times before resuming normal operations. It wasn't unusual for trips to get shuffled several times. As a result, keeping track of the vouchers became time-consuming and challenging. We needed a way to streamline the voucher system to ensure all the funds were accounted for and the proper amount was allocated. Once more I summoned our IT department and just like before, we mapped out a way to easily track a travel voucher's movements through our system.

Sometimes it takes a shake-up to initiate a shakedown of a business's operational structure. This is important to note, because if everything appears to be going well—employees are happy, sales are good, and the business is profitable—the little kinks in the system can go unnoticed. We can easily fall into a mindset of, "If it ain't broke, don't fix it." Or another classic, "We always do it this way because we've always done it this way." Maybe it's not broken, but there's always room for improvement, especially when new technology is being developed that can help us work smarter, not harder. This is why I've scheduled regular performance audits for each department. During this process I invite employees to look at why and how we operate and come up with answers to the question, "How can we make it better?" Because disruption isn't the only way to foster innovation. We can also achieve it with focus, curiosity and discipline.

KNOWNS AND UNKNOWNS

If you are ever in the position of buying an existing business, I've got two words for you: due diligence. Even if it seems like a no-brainer of a deal, use your brain and do your research. Don't let your passion get ahead of pragmatism. It pays to heed the words of Donald Rumsfeld, Secretary of Defense during the Ford and Bush administrations, who famously said, "There are known knowns, things we know that we know; and there are known unknowns, things that we know we don't know. But there are also unknown unknowns, things we do not know we don't know." This quote is from Rumsfeld's book, aptly named, *Known and Unknown*. Think about this quote for a minute and let it sink in.

I've borrowed from Rumsfeld's quote and put my own spin on it. I say, "What scares the hell out of me is what I don't know that I don't know." This kind of ignorance has big teeth and it'll bite you, mostly because it's the stuff that comes out of nowhere, when you're not expecting it.

Practically every business owner has found himself or herself getting blindsided, and later saying, "I should have seen it coming." The thing is, you can't see the unforeseen—especially when it comes to "acts of God" things like weather and a pandemic. No matter how thoroughly you've conducted your due diligence, there will always be things that come up later that you didn't know about—but all the sudden they're happening. The one thing you can do is stay alert. Pay attention. Keep a close eye on your business, especially when you're just starting out. If something's not working and you need to make a course correction, do it as quickly and efficiently as possible.

INNOVATION & LEADERSHIP STYLE

Hard times make strong leaders stronger.

ON BEING AVAILABLE

Since you can't pay attention to everything all at once, it's important to develop an open line of communication with managers and staff. Some business owners lock themselves in their offices and appoint a personal assistant or secretary to serve as a "gatekeeper" whose job is to keep employees at a distance. It's not how I operate. I don't understand business owners who do this. Maybe their egos get inflated, and they start believing their time is so precious that they can't be "bothered" by their employees. I think this is nonsense. I mean, how will you get the best performance out of your staff if you craft a reputation for being unapproachable?

Yes, there are times when I'm on a call or in a meeting and I need to work undisturbed for a while. That's normal. But being temporarily unavailable is completely different than being unapproachable and walled-off from the people who work for you.

My office door is usually open. And rather than parking behind a desk and establishing myself as unavailable/too busy, I routinely check in with the various departments in our Augusta, GA office. Instead of relying on one or two managers to provide me with operational updates, I visit each department of the company for direct reports on how things are going. By being available and approachable, I demonstrate my commitment to my business and the people who work to help make it a success. Being directly involved allows me to fully understand every aspect of the business, especially during times when we are adding new technology and upgrading our operational procedures.

My employees in our Augusta office know they are welcome in my office any time. They also know that when they come to me with a potential problem, I expect them to also come to me with at least a couple ideas on how to solve it. After all, they're the ones doing the job every day. They know I respect them enough listen and give feedback. Most importantly, it helps builds good relationships and creates a more peaceful, productive workplace.

LEARNING AS A LEADERSHIP STYLE

As a scuba diver, I continued my training from the recreational to professional level, becoming certified as an instructor. But I didn't stop there. I continued to the level of instructor trainer for two of the major global scuba training agencies. Do I spend a lot of time teaching scuba or training future scuba instructors? No. Then why would I take the time to train to these levels? I've been asked this question many times.

First, it comes down to a simple saying, "The more you know, the more you grow." This is true of both business growth and personal growth. Every business owner knows, or should know, that to grow, the business needs to always be finding new ways to improve. This is what ensures continued success. This is also true if you are an employee at a company. The way to get promoted or to secure a salary increase is to up your game.

No, I don't spend my time teaching scuba diving or training future scuba instructors. But knowing how to do these things ensures that I understand the job descriptions of the people I hire to do these jobs. This helps me hire the right people and helps me know what resources to provide so they can succeed at their jobs. Plus, it gains me greater credibility with my staff. I can literally lead by example; I can work alongside them. Because they know I understand all aspects of the job I expect them to perform, they're less likely to slack off—and more likely to shine.

I have either learned it on YouTube, read books, or taken classes pertaining to every aspect of my business. I can do basic computer programming, basic graphic design, advanced video editing, and a lot of mechanical repairs. Does this mean I do all these jobs at work? Of course not. I hire skilled staff members who do these jobs. However, my job is to have a comprehensive grasp on what my business is and how it operates.

Knowing all these things gets me excited and helps me be hyper creative. I'm constantly testing new ideas on how to move my companies to the next level. And I can tell you from experience, that excitement is contagious. When employees see the business owner or manager rolling up their sleeves and getting to work, they feel motivated. Just sitting behind the desk barking orders won't cut it. You must lead by example.

I don't know who first said, "The only constant is change," but it's true. Success isn't a finish line you cross, and then the race is over. No, you have to keep going, to keep challenging yourself to grow and change for the better. This will ultimately be the deciding factor in whether you achieve business success.

ON IDENTIFYING A MENTOR

Journalists and media people often ask me to talk about mentors who've influenced my life and career. Rather than identifying one person as a mentor, I have learned many useful bits and pieces of advice from many people over the years. That said, if I had to pick one person who was extremely influential, it would be Lt. Colonel Tony Trezza. He was my USAF Commander while at the 2nd Aeromedical Evacuation Squadron (AES) in Germany.

Every medic assigned to the 2nd AES started out working in the equipment section, which meant starting early each morning configuring all the aircraft scheduled to transport patients that day. This was an important job requiring a lot of personnel and equipment, as each aircraft was essentially a flying hospital emergency room.

Even more important was the job of scheduling, as it meant organizing the aircraft, flight and medical crews, equipment and flight routes. I was eventually selected as one of three people to staff the scheduling section. It was a big responsibility, including being on call 24/7, but it came with equally big perks, as it allowed me to oversee my flight schedule. I could handpick my flights and the crew I flew with. It also meant I had the opportunity to interact with everyone in the squadron, from top to bottom. I routinely sat in on the morning Commander's Call, during which each section within the squadron presented a status report to our commander, Lt. Col. Trezza.

It was Lt. Col. Trezza who taught me a graduate-level course on separating work from play. It turned out we both shared a love of racquetball. Almost immediately after I was assigned to the scheduling section, we started playing racquetball together every afternoon. We quickly became partners on the base racquetball team, competing with other squadrons and occasionally other bases and forts. Most days, Lt. Col. Trezza would stop by my desk before lunch and instruct me to reserve a court. In the military, rank does have its privileges, as we always got a reservation, even if it meant bumping players of lower ranking. We would routinely head over and practice for an hour, shower and then return to the squadron to finish out the day.

On the court, he treated me as an equal. Rank or status never accompanied us onto the racquetball court. We were both exceptional players and truly enjoyed our time sweating and beating up on the competition. Back at the squadron, he was an officer, and I was an enlisted. Off the court, our friendship didn't interfere with his leadership position.

I distinctly remember one Commander's Call where I learned that important lesson. In the military, seating around a commander's table is typically assigned by your position in the unit. In our meetings, Lt. Col. Trezza was seated at the head of the table with his second in command on his right. In my role as flight scheduler, I was seated on his left. That morning, I announced the list of nurses and medics whose leave requests had been approved. It is the role of the commander to approve the leave requests, and somehow Lt. Col. Trezza hadn't been provided the list for approval before I made the announcement. I don't know how the screw up happened, but what happened next was that Lt. Col. Trezza lost his temper and tore into me, asking me if I thought I was now in charge of the squadron and had given myself the authority to approve leave requests without his permission. He really let me have it. With multiple F-bombs for emphasis. All I could do was apologize for the mistake and vow that it would never happen again.

An hour or so later, Lt. Col. Trezza stopped by my office like he had done so many days before and instructed me to reserve a racquetball court for that afternoon. It was as if that morning's blow up never happened. We never spoke of it.

Sometimes you immediately recognize a learning moment and sometimes it takes a while for it to sink in. I immediately knew my response to him that morning was the appropriate action, to accept responsibility, apologize, and assure him the mistake wouldn't be repeated. Years later, when I was the business owner sitting at the head of the table berating my staff for a screw up, I had a flashback to that Commander's Call meeting. The flashback came with an epiphany. I had let my staff know in no uncertain terms that I wasn't happy, and they assured me they wouldn't let the mistake happen again. And that was the end of it. Thanks to the lesson from Lt. Col. Trezza, I knew the best course of action was to move forward. There was no need to bring it up again.

I suppose I've always thought of a mentor as a person who offers advice and guidance over a period of several years or more. Even though I wasn't under Lt. Col. Trezza's command for a long time, there's no doubt his leadership left a lasting impression on me. I suppose I would call him a mentor.

NEVER PROBLEMS, ONLY OPPORTUNITIES

I get asked A LOT how I deal with all the stress that must come with Aggressor Adventures, particularly since it's a global enterprise that operates 24/7. My answer might seem oversimplified, but I have always tried to approach it with the attitude that there are never problems, only opportunities.

Adopting this leadership style is important for those at the top, but it's just as important for everyone in the business, because it sets an example that stressing over an issue never solves it. Hysteria is contagious. So is an attitude of calm.

I always focus on what we must do to resolve a particular issue. Once that's done, I step back and review the entire event with my team. I always ask two questions: how did it happen, and what can we do in the future to prevent it from occurring again? The goal is to learn from the situation, make changes and improvements where they're needed, and then move on to the larger goal of continuing to grow the business.

Of course, there are days when I cannot believe how many "opportunities" happen all at once!

Every business owner's brain needs a break from the 24/7 hamster wheel of managing daily tasks and churning out new ideas. Some people might "veg out" by binge-watching a Netflix series or lounging by a pool or at the beach. That kind of relaxation—lying still and not moving—would feel like torture to me. I need to keep active in order clear my mind. For a recharge, I turn to personal projects like working on our motorhome or clearing land and building a fence on our property. Any project that gets me moving and requires 100 percent of my focus is like a reset button that will help me clear my mind. When I return to the office after these projects, I feel as refreshed as taking an entire week off. Of course, "off" is a misnomer. With worldwide internet and cell connectivity, an entrepreneur is never truly "off" work. I don't view this as a negative. I think it's in the DNA of an entrepreneur to want to keep their finger on the pulse of their business.

I feel grateful that my wife Dana understands this and is always supportive of my business check-ins, whether by email or phone, even when we are on vacation. Once, on a motorhome trip we stopped in a small town just to wander the streets and duck into the local shops. Upon entering a shop my cell phone rang and I saw it was a business call. I answered and motioned to Dana that I'd be outside. As I headed for the door, the shop owner commented to Dana that maybe I needed to learn to take a break from my business. Dana, without hesitation said, "He is making us money, leave him alone."

Most of my business's worldwide adventures begin and end on a Saturday, so that's also when the likelihood of problems arising is greatest. While I have an amazing, dedicated team in place to resolve issues, there are plenty of Saturdays when I get a call from a member of my operations team, alerting me to an issue or asking for guidance. If they're calling me, I know it's because they want my help. I never sigh or think "Well, shit, there goes my Saturday," before answering. And I sure as hell don't get angry about them calling me. They're doing the right thing by reaching out. If they're calling me, it means I have an opportunity to help serve our guests and make sure they enjoy the adventure they paid for.

ESTABLISHING A CLEAR TARGET

I don't have an MBA, so it might not surprise you that I don't run my businesses the way a business school graduate might. Sales forecasting is a prime example. A lot of companies spend a great deal of time, energy, and money trying to determine the total size of the market and estimate what percentage of the market they can capture. They think it's important put a lot of effort into analyzing the various factors that might impact their business.

When I've been interviewed by people from business publications, they are often shocked to learn I never forecast sales. When they ask why, I explain I have two reasons. First, there are so many variables at play. Many factors are outside of my control, or anybody's control. I pay close attention to what's happening in the world around me, but I don't obsess about things I can't change. Next, I explain I work hard every day to ensure I maximize sales. This is what's in my control. I'd rather spend my time making sales than forecasting them. I don't need a forecast or target to motivate me; my work ethic is strong without my needing to create an imaginary carrot to dangle in front of my face. Instead of aiming to hit made-up targets, I focus my energy on marketing, advertising, and providing the highest level of customer service possible.

I am excited about growing my business and I lead my team in a way that helps each person develop a work ethic like mine. I have always despised bonus plans based on sales targets. To continue with the carrot/stick analogy, I've seen bonus plans backfire, where an employee that wasn't a hard worker benefitted from a bonus scheme because of the work of others. They got a free carrot. I've also seen the opposite, where a hard worker busts their tail and then barely misses a target that was required to meet their bonus goal. They got the stick when they deserved a carrot. In either case, it's bad for business because it can bring morale down. I prefer to use customer satisfaction to incentivize exceptional service. This establishes a clear target and a winning bonus strategy. For instance, a business can develop a way to receive direct customer feedback on a staff member using a numerical ranking, then assign a dollar value to that ranking. In this way, you can track and reward excellent customer service; you'll also get an idea of which staff members' performance needs improvement. By using a merit-based bonus system rather than a made-up sales target, the business creates direct rewards and removes external factors that might otherwise impact a bonus scheme.

The bottom line is, so-called "standard business practices" aren't the only way to go. While there are some standard practices that are good to follow, but there is no blueprint for how every business should operate, so don't be afraid to step outside what most people would call is the norm. Experiment to find what works best for you and your business.

MEETING MADNESS

Early in my career as a Taco Bell franchise owner I was emailing a technology staff member at Taco Bell corporate with a question, but I never heard back from him. A week later I had a meeting at corporate headquarters, so I made sure to arrive early so I could ask him the question in person. When I arrived, I was told he was in a meeting. When I stopped by about an hour later, same thing. Another meeting. It took three more tries that day to finally find him in his office. He apologized, explaining he'd been in and out of meetings all day, as usual.

The way he said, "as usual" stuck with me. I could sense his frustration. Before I got to the question I'd originally come to ask, I asked, "Is this normal, all the meetings?" He shrugged and nodded yes. I thought, no wonder he hasn't gotten back to me. He's running the halls all day, going to meetings.

Then I asked him if he'd seen my email. I was standing beside his desk as he said no, but he'd check. I could see his email program was open and I couldn't help but notice he had 400 unread emails! He searched for mine, read it, and finally answered the question I'd been waiting over a week to have answered. He apologized for the delay, and admitted that if I hadn't shown up, he'd probably never have gotten around to reading my email.

I know a lot of us get more email than we should, but that is the world we live in. Still, no email should ever go unanswered because you were in too many meetings. "I'm too busy" isn't an excuse. It's a problem that needs solving.

There are good reasons for holding meetings. Unfortunately, most companies overdo it. If you are meeting daily, you've got a problem. Even an hour-long weekly meeting may not seem like that much time out of a week, but you must consider the time your staff uses reviewing the notes from the last meeting, prepping for the upcoming meeting and then organizing the notes from the current meeting.

Here are some guidelines for scheduling and leading meetings. First, the only reason you should have a meeting is to discuss an ongoing project. Only those directly involved in the project should attend, and each person should arrive ready to update others on their progress. One person should be tasked with running the meeting, while another serves as a note-taker. At the start, provide an overview of the project from the last time the team met. Next, each person should be given a couple minutes to update the team on their progress and note any areas where they might need help. Once this is done, allow a few minutes for idea-sharing and collaboration, highlighting any of the team members' requests for input. Lastly, take a couple minutes to identify the project's next steps, and remind everyone of the timeline. After the meeting wraps, the note-taker should email attendees with meeting highlights. You might be surprised, but when you stay focused, you can get all this done in less than an hour—often less than half an hour.

Don't hold meetings just to spread information. If you are updating your staff on a project without inviting feedback, then a meeting is probably a waste of everyone's time This "information sharing" meeting is what I see on most companies' calendars. It's a waste of everyone's time and talent. Instead, send that information in an email.

Email was intended to make us hyper productive, and it can, but only if everyone is allowed the time to keep up with it. I can absorb about 100 emails a day. There's no way I could attend 100 meetings in a day, or even a week. I allow each of my departments to have no more than ONE meeting a week (or fewer, if they don't need to meet). I also define a department very broadly, so they do not end up with such project-specific meetings that we end up with multiple meetings under the same department umbrella.

Meetings, whether in person or by video, are essential. But remember, this is time that needs managing, not wasting. It is much easier to call a meeting to discuss a project rather than to work on the project. The last thing you want is to have employees appear busy without their getting any real work done. When you set clear guidelines for your company and staff on why to call a meeting, who should attend, and how it should be structured, you are increasing your company's productivity, not limiting it.

MANAGING MEETINGS AND WORKFLOW

Owning a worldwide, multi-destination business is perfect for my ever-churning brain. I absolutely love to learn. I regularly take classes on extremely varied topics, and I enjoy reading technical documents and watching documentaries that in some way relate to my work. Still, owning a global business has forced me to make some important changes to my daily routine.

When I started in the restaurant business, my focus was rather narrow compared to what it is now. I checked my email each morning for exception reports my software generated and kept an eye on local and national economic forecasts. These days, I start my day by checking currency valuations from at least 10 countries in which we do business. When currency valuations fluctuate, it can have a direct impact on our bookings. Sometimes it requires us to get more creative with our marketing initiatives.

I also subscribe to online newspapers from our top destinations so I can keep an eye on their economic and political outlook as well. The pandemic added an entire new set of matrixes I had to follow, which changed almost daily. The other significant difference from my restaurant days is that because we operate in every time zone in the world, I routinely wake up to a full email inbox. While I have my first cup of coffee I sort through my emails, answering most right away and flagging others for follow up later in the day.

On weekdays you'll usually find me at our headquarters, where my staff and I handle the day-to-day business. I reserve Tuesdays for meetings with all my departments. I know a lot of business owners like to schedule meetings on Mondays, but I've found Tuesdays to be more productive, as it gives everyone a chance to reset after the weekend and handle any follow ups from the previous week. I start with Operations and move on to IT, Conservation and Outreach, Marketing and Advertising and end with our Boutique and Production department. Even though it can make for a long day (and normally lunch at my desk), scheduling the meetings this way ensures I have the remainder of the week to devote to the various projects we cover in our meetings.

One of my favorite tasks is combing through the stack of "prospects" I keep on my desk. It's a compilation of potential new destinations up for consideration. Some take years to develop, while others move from idea to up and running relatively quickly. I enjoy this a lot, as it's exciting to envision new and exciting destinations that will help satisfy our guests' passion for adventure.

I usually end my day returning guest phone calls and emails. I find that if I try to tackle those first thing in the day, I am too distracted to give them my full attention. Of course, there are exceptions; if they are in a time zone that is many hours different from mine, I sometimes must make those calls at 4 am instead of 4 pm. I'm not complaining, though. It's all a part of owning a business that operates around the clock.

Rather than look at email and phone calls as a burden or distraction, I see it as allowing me to have the most productivity I could ever imagine! I can and often do work from all over the world, thanks to reliable internet access and cell phone service.

Of course, owning and running Aggressor Adventures would not be complete without me spending time with our guests. I try to schedule at least three guest trips a year. Not only do I love the travel and adventure (and of course, the diving), but I also value spending a week with guests where I can get their feedback and input. We get some great ideas from our guests, and we're always looking for new ideas that will improve the customer experience. Paying close attention to customer feedback is essential for any business that wants to continue to grow and expand.

I am often asked about my retirement plans. My honest answer is always that I have no plans to retire! It is an absolute pleasure going to the office, working with such a great team and providing our guests with their adventure fixes. Besides, my brain would implode if I ever tried to shut it off!

BECOMING AN EXPERT

recently was asked to appear on an hour-long podcast during which I'd be introduced as an expert on Sri Lanka and its safari tourism. Aggressor Adventures operates in Sri Lanka, and of course I know a lot about the country and its natural resources, but I would have never cast myself as an expert. However, when an opportunity arises to promote my business, I'm always all in, so I spent several days researching and making notes about Sri Lanka in general, its national parks specifically, and why travelers might want to visit the country on safari. I also did a little a bit of research on the podcast host and listened to a few podcasts to get a feel for what to expect.

I studied the "Big Five" animals safari visitors hope to see, which include the Asian elephant, leopard, sloth bear, mugger crocodile, and wild oxen. I soaked up details on these animals' average like weights, diets, habitats and ranges, populations, endangered status and interesting behaviors. Since our safaris operate in two of the national parks, I researched why and how the parks were established and learned about the flora and fauna.

I did the same with the country's history and culture. Before I started learning about the country, I vaguely knew that Sri Lanka's recent history included a period of political unrest. It turns out the government had mandated organic farming without first determining if their regulations would foster a sustainable or economically feasible program. Sadly, the results were catastrophic. Low crop yields caused economic ruin and food instability, driving the country's population to the brink of starvation. This sparked riots that led to the ouster of the sitting president and forced a new election.

It might seem like I went a little overboard preparing to be a guest on a podcast. In fact, my time was well spent. The podcast has a huge following, most of whom live in the USA's farm belt. The interviewer was thrilled that I could speak about Sri Lanka's diverse animal life while also offering listeners commentary on the effects of the country's failed agricultural initiatives. The podcast was a big success, with high engagement and a lot of positive feedback.

My point is that I might not consider myself an expert on Sri Lanka, its safaris or its history of political and social challenges, but with a bit of research I was able to hold my own in an hour-long podcast. It all comes down to preparation. I had a chance to advertise my business to potential customers, so I jumped on it. And you can do the same. It's all a matter of taking initiative and making the best of the opportunities that come your way.

ATTITUDE & ADAPTABILITY

If it was easy, everyone would do it. There will be tough times that test you; it's just part of life as an entrepreneur.

MAKING THE RIGHT HIRE

knew that just giving managers and employees my definition of success was not going to achieve it; I needed to develop and implement a plan to get there.

When I was just starting out as a manager, I found the toughest challenge was hiring staff that was friendly, smiled and engaged with our customers. I wanted them to deliver great customer service. I was not satisfied with mediocre customer service. I wanted to have customers seek me out to say how great they were treated at every one of my Taco Bell locations. That was my definition of success for that business. Yes, profit was important. But I knew if my customers were happy, profit would follow.

When I first started interviewing and hiring people, my biggest challenge was getting a clear picture of the candidate and whether they would be a good fit or not. I mean, people who want a job are likely to say what they think you want to hear, right? After conducting many interviews and hirings, I eventually found my groove. I started to understand what to look for in a good hire.

You've probably heard the phrase, "attitude is everything." I hadn't given it much thought, but it turns out to be 100 percent true. I have learned that you can train anyone to do just about anything, but the most difficult thing is to change their attitude. And in some instances, you can't change their attitude.

A person's overall attitude during the interview is the most important thing. I discovered that a candidate's age, education, or previous employment experience was dwarfed by a positive or negative attitude. I quit listening to the answers they gave to the questions I asked. Instead, I paid attention to how they entered the room, if they looked me in the eye, and what their body language and facial expressions might reveal. Having someone say they are a "people person" who is very good at customer service doesn't mean anything if they can't back it up with a positive attitude—their overall vibe.

I quickly realized when I started to grow my Taco Bell franchise that my store managers were likely to have the same interviewing challenges I'd experienced. I created a mini course for them I taught called Border Attitude, which referenced Taco Bell's successful "Run for the Border" advertising campaign. It focused on the individual job candidate's attitude during the interview more than their skill set or previous employment history. I wanted the manager to get a feel for them—would this person's attitude create a positive vibe as a new member of the store team? If the answer was yes, hire them and give them a try. If not, move on to the next candidate.

I also cautioned my managers that filling a position with a person who was wrong for the job was worse than leaving that position open. Why? Because every business is judged by its worst employee. Customers are likely to forgive slow service if they see everyone working hard and being friendly. One thing they won't likely forgive is a poor attitude. If they aren't treated kindly, they'll take their money someplace else.

If I pulled up to one of my stores and saw a new cashier that I hadn't met, I would approach the register as a typical customer and see how I was greeted. That was always going to be the best test of how real customers were being handled and if the manager was making good hires.

I still use this interview practice today. Some positions within Aggressor Adventures require specific qualifications, like a captain or engineer. Even though these jobs require skills and experience, the right attitude is what gets a potential new hire across the line. Or out the door.

ADAPTING AGGRESSIVELY

Every long-term entrepreneur knows that there are prosperous times and lean times in any business. During the lean times, businesses must adapt or die. Aggressor Fleet was born out of the need to adapt to challenging times.

Paul Haines was a lifelong shipyard owner and boat captain. He operated a fleet of commercial vessels used to ferry crew and supplies to offshore oil rigs located in the waters off the southeastern United States. During the oil bust of the early 1980s, he found himself with several crew vessels tied to his shipyard dock, idle. He had no work, but the bank still wanted their monthly loan payments, so Paul had to come up with a way to monetize the crew boats. An avid scuba diver, he came up with the idea of remodeling the smallest crew vessel to accommodate divers who could charter the boat for a week at a time for diving adventures. He had a fondness for the Cayman Islands and decided it would be the perfect location to test this new liveaboard concept. Paul always named his vessels "aggressive" names that began with C/ for his shipyard name, Comer Marine. He had boats with names like *C/Conqueror* and *C/Dominator*. His smallest vessel was named *C/Aggressor*. It was easy enough to change the C/ to Cayman. This is how the *Cayman Aggressor* got its name.

Obviously, Paul's plan worked. It was successful enough that he remodeled another vessel a couple of years later. Soon, the former crew vessels had become the Aggressor Fleet of liveaboard dive yachts. Before long he began licensing the name and company's SOPs. Paul cleverly reallocated his resources in an economic downturn, and in the process created an innovative license concept that saved his company and made him a lot of money.

I admired and respected the sacrifices Paul made during those difficult years, and how he got creative with his physical assets. As the new owner of Aggressor Fleet, I wanted to make all the right choices going forward, to honor what he'd built.

After buying the company, I traveled to each destination (there were eight at that time) around the world to see the yachts and meet the owners and crews whose amazing service had had enticed me to purchase the company in the first place. I was excited to build on the success of Paul Haines' vision and spent my first year of ownership reorganizing and refining practically every part of the company.

As I expanded into new scuba diving liveaboard destinations, in the back of my mind I was always looking to expand into non-diving adventure businesses. This would grow my potential customer base beyond scuba divers and snorkelers. Essentially, every traveler in the world could be a customer. It wasn't long before a very forward-thinking Licensee, David Home, inquired about adding a Nile River cruise and a Sri Lanka Safari Lodge. I was all in, and another adaptation of Aggressor was born! What started as Comer Marine crew boats became the Aggressor Fleet of liveaboard dive yachts, and now Aggressor Fleet has grown into Aggressor Adventures.

TAKING THE FEAR OUT OF FAILING

In every business, you never truly know the outcome of a new change until it has been fully implemented and given time to either succeed or fail. However, even the failures should be viewed as a form of success.

When the 2008 financial crisis hit and in early 2009 began rebounding, I was looking for ways to make my company stand out from my competitors and turn the recent economic downturn into a win for my company. I decided to hire two salespeople to travel North America making sales calls to dive centers. We came up with mini seminars designed to educate store owners on how much profit they could make by booking their customers onto one of my liveaboards. Our sales team also taught them how to promote our trips to their clients.

We agreed to test the initiative for a year, expecting to see an uptick in bookings from the stores they visited. They did a great job meeting dive store owners, and their presentations were informative and engaging. We received positive feedback from the dive centers, too. What didn't we see? We didn't see sales go up. In fact, the program didn't bring in enough revenue to cover their salaries. We were losing money.

After the year was up, we all knew and had to accept that this program wasn't working, so I eliminated both positions. They completely understood—it was business and not personal—and we parted ways on good terms, as friends.

Once you've pulled the plug, be sure to examine what might have caused an idea to fail. It's important to learn what went wrong and figure out why. The findings are crucial in ensuring you do not repeat the same mistakes in the future.

Tracking some forms of marketing, like billboards, radio or television ads can be hard to quantify. For a direct sales approach like this program where you hire salespeople for a specific target, it is easy to determine the results.

Analyzing the failure of any part of your business turns that failure into potential success. Never be afraid to try something new once you have outlined its potential for successful. If it does fail, don't let that failure deter you from trying new ideas in the future. If you ask a highly successful entrepreneur about their failures, they'll probably admit they have a lot of stories they could tell.

RUTHLESS VERSUS REALISTIC

I recently had a very interesting conversation with one of my competitors, during which we were discussing different destinations and how we manage profitability at each one. And he said, "I've noticed over the years, you're pretty ruthless about shutting one [a Licensee] down." I responded by saying, "I don't think of it as being ruthless; I see it as living in reality."

If one of our License destinations, or any business, or a division of a business is not making a profit, it's important to filter out your emotions and address the problem objectively. This is where making decisions based on the numbers will always be best. As you analyze the profit/loss data and you see you're in the red, it's important to look for reasons why things aren't going in the right direction. This is when you might need to put a little emotion into it (I know, I just said don't do this) because maybe what your business needs is a little kick in the backside, a bit of motivation and a fresh approach to help turn things around. The key is to avoid getting too emotionally attached to the outcome—and don't ever think you are personally a failure because part of your business is not successful.

Think of it like a tree; sometimes you need to trim the dead wood from a few branches, but you don't need to dig the whole tree up by the roots. Give yourself a set amount of time and attention to the turnaround effort. Look at what hasn't been working and try something different. If it still isn't working, if it's not pulling a profit, then it's time to make a very good business decision to shut it down. Remember, making a responsible business decision has nothing to do with you being a failure as a person. Recognizing failure is the first success. Every successful entrepreneur has tried and failed. What matters is that you keep trying.

DON'T BE A KNOW-IT-ALL

Just because you've learned a thing or two, doesn't mean that everyone who works with you or for you has learned the same lessons. It's important to keep things in perspective and not come off like a know-it-all who is quick to dismiss others' ideas.

This requires patience, but it's important to meet people where they are. There have been times when my staff members came to me saying they're ready to complete the next step in their plan for success, but when they shared the plan, I felt sure it wasn't fully thought out. In fact, there have been times when I felt it was going to fail. Sometimes I have allowed a plan like this to move forward despite my concerns. Why? For one, maybe they can prove me wrong. Maybe they're coming at it from a different angle, and they see something I haven't yet noticed. Secondly, I know that learning by failing will likely teach them important lessons. Obviously, I won't approve a plan that would potentially endanger people or in some other way cause damage, but there are times when a cautious "wait and see" approach is possible. In cases like this, I keep an open mind and keep a close eye on their progress. If their plan succeeds, great. If not, we quickly refocus and move forward.

Failure can be a catalyst for growth. Businesses that succeed have figured out how to remove the stigma from failure and encourage their employees to show initiative.

As a side note, there are times when some of your steps to success will seem overwhelming, but if what you are doing is worth it, stick with it. Don't give up just because it gets hard, or you feel tired. Instead of giving up, step back for a moment and catch your breath. I know the old adage, "When the going gets tough, the tough get going" gets overused, but there's truth in it. Never skip one step just because it's hard, because these steps often turn out to be the most rewarding.

MEETING PEOPLE WHERE THEY ARE

Earlier, I wrote about how profoundly affected I was by the birth of my son Justin. I was amazed at how fatherhood completely changed my perspective on life. When we found out we were pregnant with our second child, we hoped for a girl, and we were thrilled when our daughter Ashley was born. Since I'd already had the life-changing experience of fatherhood, I hadn't expected to be overwhelmed with emotion, but it happened again. When I held Ashley for the first time, the same flood of love and joy and awe washed over me. My desire to be a loving, protective parent just doubled.

We got plenty of parenting advice with the births of each of our kids. One thing we didn't pay attention to after Ashley's birth was any, "raise boys like this and girls like that" tips from well-meaning friends. We aimed to foster their independence and their individuality, so we tried to avoid treating our son and daughter differently based on their gender. Dana and I agreed we wanted to raise strong-willed individuals who knew how to think with their heads and their hearts. We wanted them to believe that with determination and perseverance, they could achieve any goal they set.

Despite our goal to support their individualism, we sort of figured that two children from the same parents, living in the same house, eating the same food and going through the same daily routines, would be similar. We could not have been more wrong. It turns out our kids didn't need our help with their individualism, because each is their own person and they're as different as night and day.

Justin is happy to fly by the seat of his pants, succeeding by winging it along the way. Ashley is more of a planner. She practices and prepares for flawless execution.

Ashley recently participated in a fund-raising dance competition,

Dancing Stars of Augusta, a Dancing With the Stars-type event sponsored by the Alzheimer's Association®. She practiced her dance routine for months and really gave it her all, which earned her both the People's Choice Award and Judge's Choice Award for her performance. She also raised nearly 50,000 dollars in support of Alzheimer's research.

I'm sharing this story partly as a humble brag on my daughter's recent success, but also to offer this advice to business managers: meet people where they are. The people working in your company might be "living in the same house, eating the same food and going through the same daily routines" but they are individuals. Each comes pre-wired with their own operating system. When you take a minute to figure out how an employee operates, you can harness their innate ability in a way that benefits them and helps grow your company.

MINDING YOUR MINDSET

Since the start of Aggressor Adventures in 1984, our guests and dive staff have accumulated millions of dives. When I first started scuba diving, there was a brief period during which I was eager to log as many dives as possible. I'll admit that for a while, I got a little hooked on filling logbooks. Once I weaned myself off the goal of reaching another diving milestone, I found each dive more enjoyable. I learned that the most important statistic is how much I enjoyed the dive rather than what number dive it was.

It turns out I'm not the only diver who has ever been mildly obsessed with dive numbers. I was onboard a dive yacht in the Caribbean a few years ago when a buddy team proudly shared with me that they had completed 10 of the five dives offered on the first day of the cruise. It seems they were going to their planned depth, spending 15 minutes and then coming to the surface for 15 minutes and then descending once more for another 15 minutes—just so they could count one dive as two. They were spending all their bottom time looking at their time computers instead of enjoying the underwater scenery. During that one outing they'd missed seeing the eagle ray, sea turtles and the large nurse shark. I encouraged them to rethink their mission and their mindset, otherwise they would be missing out on all the amazing sea life in exchange for a number in a dive log.

I am not suggesting that divers quit logging their dives or celebrating their milestone dives, but I encourage our guests to enjoy the excitement of each dive they make with us. I love being onboard with a guest that is excited to reach a milestone number, like their 100th or 500th dive, but I'm just as excited to hear divers' stories of seeing a shark for the first time or making their first night dive. There are so many "firsts" we get to experience.

Onboard Aggressor yachts, we celebrate every guest who completes every dive offered during a week long cruise with a special Iron Diver award. We never heavily promote it or push it, but we like to offer special recognition for those guests who want to enjoy every dive offered. Notice I said "enjoy" every dive. I never want any of our guests to feel compelled to complete every dive. It's their vacation. We want them to enjoy it. My personal experience has taught me that there's something to enjoy on every dive, no matter what the number. I hope all our diving guests will log their dive memories and let the number of dives be a distant thought that never distracts from their passion for scuba diving.

I think this mindset applies to growing a business, too. For instance, when I was adding Taco Bell locations to my business, it would have been easy to focus solely on hitting a target number of new stores. But in doing so, I could have been distracted from the joy of the development process, or most importantly, the profitability of the planned location.

VISION & STRATEGY

You can't save your way to success, but you can spend your way into bankruptcy. Balancing the two is a constant challenge.

AVOIDING THE CASTLE MENTALITY

Owning or managing a business that has more than one location presents a unique set of challenges when it comes to uniformity and consistency. This is especially true of a multi-destination business like Aggressor Adventures. Customers expect a particularly high level of service at each Aggressor destination, no matter where in the world it is located, and it's up to the local staff to deliver.

If you have your own business with more than one location or supervise multiple locations for an employer, it's important to schedule regular check-ins and site visits. Otherwise, it can be easy for the manager at that site to forget they are part of a larger network. They can start to feel alone or isolated. When this happens, managers may tend to think and act independently instead of following the Standard Operating Procedures of your company. This is what I call Castle Mentality.

I don't know it it's ego or just human nature, but I've seen Castle Mentality, a lot. Without regular supervision, management staff, no matter how dedicated or hard working, will behave as if they have their own kingdom; they tend to start running the castle how they see fit instead of according to your company's policies. This is where customer service standards can go south, putting your entire enterprise at risk.

In 1986 the NASA space shuttle *Challenger* exploded 73 seconds into its flight, killing all seven astronaut crew members aboard. The launch was broadcast on live television. Viewers watched in horror, wondering, "How in the world could this have happened?" When experts were investigating what caused the catastrophic failure of the spacecraft, they identified "normalization of deviance" as the root cause. Normalization of deviance happens when individuals, groups or organizations come to accept a lower standard of performance until that lower standard becomes the "norm" for them. This usually occurs when individuals, groups or organizations are under pressure to meet schedule requirements, conform to budgetary considerations or deliver on a promise, while adhering to expected standards or prescribed procedures. When under pressure, they decide to utilize lower standards "just this once" with the expectation that when things get back to "normal" they will go back to utilizing the higher standards or procedures.

I think you can see where this is going. Every time a corner gets cut, the standard gets lowered and soon, the high standard gets forgotten. Again, to keep your business running by the book, meaning the carefully outlined SOPs, stay in regular contact, reminding them they are part of a larger network or team with high standards that must be met. Regular check-ins by phone and video conferencing are important but they cannot replace in-person site visits. When you visit in person you can get a strong sense of what's working and what's not. When I visit a location, I stick to the objective of ensuring operations are running smoothly. I make sure to bring copies of customer surveys and comment cards we can go over together. I make sure to point out areas in which they are succeeding instead of only addressing problem areas. This builds trust and helps your managers feel they are being supported. If they do have problems, they'll be more inclined to ask for help if they know you have their back.

Still, even with frequent visits and communications, some of your best and brightest may fall victim to their own self-motivation by deviating from the SOP and implementing changes without asking permission or running an idea by you. This is not a knock on your best and brightest, but an unfortunate outcome with some highly motivated employees. There must be a balance of leading while also following the program. When they think they can do it better than you by doing it their way, often the best thing you can do is help them recognize it might be time for them to move along and go do their thing someplace else.

LOOKING OUT FOR THE INDUSTRY

I follow the financial markets, inflation numbers, and real estate markets around the world to hopefully see financial trends early, before any big fluctuations occur that might negatively impact my business.

That said, the 2007-2008 global financial crisis caused major upheaval across all areas of business, including scuba diving and liveaboard dive travel. Fortunately, Aggressor Adventures appeals to higher net worth individuals who fared well enough to continue their travel plans during a turbulent economy. This meant we had an insignificant blip in sales in 2009, but business recovered back to double-digit sales growth by 2010. Our continued growth was due in large part to customers of all income levels who are loyal to our brand. Some might have held off on booking for a while, but as soon as they were ready to resume traveling, they booked with us.

Not all liveaboard operators weathered the financial storm as well as we did. A competitor with two liveaboards in the Caribbean tightened its budget by deferring regular maintenance to its yachts. This is often an early indicator of company-wide financial issues. Soon, social media forums had numerous posts about poor conditions onboard. One yacht had to cancel its scheduled trips and go into dry dock for repairs. It was rumored to have been abandoned in the shipyard.

Not long after, the company had a promotion for a "cash discount" on trips onboard its remaining yacht. Guests who paid cash would receive a significant discount. I was trying to wrap my head around how that promotion benefited the company and its clients. My ears always perk up when I see a company try marketing strategies that are outside the norm. I like companies that think outside the box, but this one didn't make much sense.

It wasn't long before the company went bust. Many of those who'd paid cash for a future trip were left with no money, and no dive vacation.

I was not going to let the liveaboard industry get a black eye due to the misdeeds of an owner that put the screws to his customers while trying to save his own hide. I immediately put out a press release in every scuba diving publication, stating that I would honor the now-defunct operator's bookings. Aggressor would credit the lost payments to any trip with my company.

While there was certainly some potential to earn lifelong customers, my primary motivation was to see that those liveaboard divers who got screwed over didn't decide to give up on liveaboard diving. I wanted to redeem our industry. In the end, I absorbed well over $100,000 in payments customers had made to the now-defunct business. I was thankful to have weathered the 2007-2008 financial crisis with the cash reserves to do so. I got calls from so many of those customers, thanking me for jumping in to help them, including a Boy Scouts group that had held multiple fund raisers to pay for their trip with the other company.

I try to always look at the long game in business. I know that sometimes the payoff will be years coming, but nevertheless, it's worth the upfront investment. The liveaboard industry did in fact avoid the black eye that would have turned customers away. I know I also gained some goodwill, as many of those divers have become longtime repeat customers. They repaid my kindness with their loyalty. It's win-win.

This story isn't intended as a blueprint for how you should operate. You must evaluate this type of situation based on your company's financial strength, the potential fallout from a bankrupt competitor, and of course, the size of the failing company. However, as an entrepreneur, it is imperative that if one of your competitors fails, you need to be looking at the potential negative impact on your business as well as how you might turn their loss into your gain.

REWARDING LOYALTY

Who doesn't want to be a member of a club? It's human nature to want to be included, especially if we're offered a chance to join a club that has a certain level of exclusivity. It makes us feel special. After my first year owning Aggressor Adventures (then known as Aggressor Fleet), I started thinking about creating exclusive clubs as part of the business. Club membership is a common strategy used across multiple business platforms, including hotels and airlines, and sports clubs like tennis and golf. Even fashion retailers utilize exclusive club memberships to offer perks to loyal customers.

When a business uses the strategy of "rewards club" memberships, the goal is to incentivize repeat business by offering perks and rewards to loyal customers/club members. For it to work, you've got to balance attainability and exclusivity. If you set the bar too low, the club won't feel special; too high and you might accidentally ward off customers who feel it's out of their reach. Again, you want your club members feeling like they're being welcomed into an elite, exclusive group of very special people.

A great way to address this is to create a network of multi-tiered clubs. Envision it like a pyramid; wider at the base and narrow at the top. The bottom tier is the base, or entry-level club. Make this first level relatively easy—but not too easy—to reach. Next, craft your clubs with increasingly challenging membership requirements, each tier offering greater, more attractive rewards that will entice your lower-tier club members to keep reaching for elite status.

To make this work for your business, consider how you will structure the rewards so that members truly feel rewarded. For instance, when an Aggressor Adventures customer achieves entry into one of my exclusive clubs, we send them a hand signed, framed club membership certificate, a welcome and thank-you letter, and an attractive gift. Our customers routinely send photos of themselves, smiling and proudly holding their certificates. We've got hundreds of these photos. It's the best proof of concept a business can get! When your customers thank you for thanking them, you know it's working.

As of this writing, I have six different clubs available to my customers. The VIP Club is open to customers who've completed 15 adventures with us. The VIP+ Club has a threshold of 25 adventures. In addition to the framed certificate, these club members also receive a gift of a rolling travel bag that has the VIP+ logo embroidered on the front, which they can use on a trip to proudly share their status with fellow travelers.

The All Star Club is an annual membership offered to customers who travel with us three or more times in a calendar year. Each year, nearly 100 of our most valued customers reach this status—with several logging their three trips in the first quarter of the year. We proudly display their names on the "Club Wall" page of our website. We sometimes have prospective All Stars who contact us right after they finish that third trip, excitedly asking when they'll see their name on the "Club Wall." This is exactly the kind of passion we want to continue to foster. And reward. It reminds us that we're on the right track with the clubs, and with customer satisfaction.

Some of our most loyal customers are those who set out to travel all around the world with my company, and I wanted to reward those that seek out some of my more remote adventure locations. I divided up the world in to Seven Seas, based on the oceanic trade routes used by early sailors. It also includes any land or river-based locations in the region. As the requirements for entry into these clubs becomes harder to achieve, the rewards become more appropriate. When you are setting up or tweaking existing clubs for your company, always build the rewards around how exclusive the club is. Your customers will see this and appreciate the acknowledgment you have created for them.

Exclusive clubs are not only a way to reward your best customers but also an incentive for repeat business or even expanded use of your different parts of your company. Since Aggressor Adventures was initially setup as a scuba diving company for the first 28 years of its existence, most of my customers are interested in my scuba diving liveaboards. To incentivize them to expand the use of other non-scuba diving adventures I offer, I created the Aggressor Adventurer Club. This exclusive club rewards customers that travel on three of the four sub-brands that I offer. Many of my customers that achieve entry into this club do so with a "back-to-back" travel plan. For example, they go on an Aggressor Red Sea scuba diving liveaboard one week then hop over to my Aggressor River Cruise on the Nile the next week.

We recently celebrated 40 years in business and while looking for ways to celebrate this amazing target for any business, I looked at everything that could be tied to the number 40. We offered special 40 percent travel discounts, and we gave 40-year logo merchandise to our best resellers. I decided to search our database to see how many customers had been on 40 or more adventures with us. I was delighted to see there were over a dozen customers! This warranted a club!

For my exclusive club honoring my customers that have been on 40 or more adventures, I wanted a name that would showcase their incredible support. I knew and had traveled with many of these customers over the years. They always spoke highly of the adventures they had been on and of the staff at each one. They were always spreading the word about Aggressor Adventures to their friends. These loyal customers are ambassadors for my company. It's only fitting we name their exclusive club the Aggressor Adventures Ambassador Club.

Rewarding repeat customers for their loyalty should be a no-brainer for every company. When setting up your clubs, make sure you take the time to be thoughtful of the rewards you give out. Ramping up the rewards based on the more they have spent with you will only encourage more repeat business and create ambassadors for more word-of-mouth business. Having happy customers do your marketing for you is highest honor a business can achieve.

LEARNING TO READ PEOPLE

One of the most valuable tools you can use to achieve success is to learn how to read people. I vividly recall my early days as city manager for Taco Bell. I was new at interviewing. On my first day of work, I interviewed five people. The interviews went well enough I guess, but I came away unsure if any of them were good candidates for the job. This was partly due to my interview style. I hadn't framed the questions to get useful responses from the candidates. I also wondered if I had been hearing the truth, or if the candidates were just telling me what they thought I wanted to hear.

Since providing excellent customer service is how I define success, and people are a key component of the service industry, I realized I needed to learn more about how to read people. It's an important skill. If you don't believe me, stop and do a quick Internet search of, "how to read people." The results will send you down a deep, fascinating rabbit hole.

In my quest to become an expert at reading people, I read books on the topic, took a class, and sought the advice of a mentor. I began practicing and paying attention, and in time I did become an expert at reading people. Now, after all these years, I can usually get a read on a person in a matter of minutes. I'm not certain the adage, "First impressions are lasting impressions" rings true every time, but I'll tell you what: first impressions are important. It's better to make a good first impression than to end up begging for a second chance.

SWIMMING VERSUS WALKING ON WATER

Another important lesson I learned about hiring people is that not every position needs to be filled with "the best of the best." This might seem counterintuitive, because of course you only want the very best employees, right? Let me explain.

If you hire a team of leaders, you've got no followers. Hire all followers, and you've got no leaders. This oversimplifies my point, but the key is to carefully match the employee with the position.

In my Taco Bell ownership days, I learned to looked for most of my store managers to be what I described as "good swimmers." These are the team members who are comfortable in the deep end and can keep swimming along just fine—they're not in over their heads and drowning. Those who came in already able to walk on water were the ones likely aiming for rapid advancement to a higher-level position. I knew that if I did not have more challenging positions open for them, they probably wouldn't stick around. The time and money I spent training them might be lost, and I'd end up right back where I started in the hiring process.

Now, with my high-end, small group adventure business, I need more employees who can walk on water, because each employee must be the exceptionally talented and capable, staff who can deliver guest service at the highest levels, consistently.

Practically every organization has a range of jobs that need to be performed. The key is to select the employee who can perform the job well at their present level of competence, and who can be trained and incentivized to increase their skill set over time. This has many advantages: it saves you time and money that would otherwise be lost to recruiting and training new hires, it fosters employee longevity and stability within your company, and it creates the opportunity for you to promote from within.

Another advantage to creating a workplace that invites longevity is that your employees can form strong professional and personal bonds. One of the best compliments an employer can ever receive is having an employee say they feel that their employer and co-workers are like family. I'm proud that Aggressor Adventures has built this reputation with our team.

DON'T PANIC, PIVOT

Every entrepreneur knows there will be ups and downs in business. We analyze economic trends to predict the future. Nearing the end of 2019, I doubt anyone predicted we'd soon be experiencing a pandemic that brought the world to a standstill. We had ZERO customers traveling, which meant ZERO revenue. I had navigated downturns in my businesses over the years, but I hadn't dealt with a challenge of this magnitude.

I started by researching the last global pandemic, which was the Spanish Flu outbreak in February of 1918. It last about 15 months, so I used that as a timeline, hoping the advances of modern medicine would curtail it sooner. No matter what the timeline, I had to ensure we took care of our 25,000 customers with existing travel reservations. Not only were we trying to reschedule 25,000 existing customers, but we had thousands more who were hopeful the travel restrictions would be quickly lifted, who still wanted to book their trips. Suddenly, we were busier than we had ever been! I assured all my staff that no one was at risk of losing their job, and to just take care of our customers.

The next big issue was customer engagement. Our clients couldn't travel, and since we didn't know when restrictions would lift, we couldn't actively market new trips to them. So, I created the Customer Engagement Initiative. The goal was to come up with new ways to stay in front of our customers and keep them engaged. I'm proud to say the entire Aggressor Adventures team excelled at this initiative!

Zoom calls became a big thing. We started with live video calls with many of our captains around the world. We interviewed them, asking about their backgrounds, how they ended up sometimes halfway around the world as a captain, and so on. We included a Q&A session, giving participants a chance to engage with the captains. We added programs with interesting celebrities like Survivorman Les Stroud, artist and conservationist Guy Harvey and others. Before long we discovered that the live video calls had a high percentage of drop-offs, so we switched to recording them and then releasing them on our social media channels for our customers to watch at their leisure. This worked, and our viewing numbers stayed strong.

Another popular engagement tool was a website treasure hunt. We would "hide" a gift item somewhere on our website and give out one hint a day to help web visitors find it. The first person to email us with the correct location of the gift won a prize such as scuba gear or boutique items. This led to our having online sweepstakes for much larger, more expensive items like free trips, dive computers and $500 vouchers. Participants had various ways in which to gain a sweepstakes entry. They could watch a new destination video, follow our Facebook page, refer a friend to our mailing list, and more. Each time they engaged with us they earned an entry. It was a huge success, with about 3,000 customers taking part—and 9 million to 12 million sweepstakes entries per sweepstakes offer! In addition to its success as a customer engagement tool, the initiative was a lot of fun, for our staff and for our customers.

We decided to broaden our focus beyond scuba diving and travel, so we created e-newsletters with categories including Foodie, Tech, Mechanical, Apps, Pet Tips, Joke of the Day and others. We got creative. We had some of our chefs share recipes or talk about their favorite kitchen gadgets. Our engineers gave advice on topics like keeping your car batteries in top shape, and our tech team shared info on the best cell phone apps. It was all about customer engagement, so Aggressor Adventures stayed on their minds while we waited for travel restrictions to lift.

We also partnered with scuba training agencies to highlight their online training options. They would give away a $300 future travel voucher with Aggressor Adventures for every online course their customers signed up for. We also partnered with scuba gear manufacturers to include a $300 Aggressor Adventures voucher with the purchase of a new dive computer. We quickly realized we had endless ways to stay in front of our existing and future customers by creating these incentives.

Many of our destinations are heavily dependent on tourism as a primary revenue source. After three months, some of our destinations' governments realized that widespread unemployment would likely drive their population into poverty and possibly bankrupt their country. We didn't wait to see that happen, so we spent countless hours developing ways to ensure the safety of those working in the tourist sector as well as those who wished to travel. We created the "Clean, Refresh and Sanitize" program. It eventually became a 99-page manual covering everything from safe handling of our customers' arrival at the destination airport, to their departure a week later. One of the biggest challenges was finding sanitizing products locally that met our own and the destination's guidelines for effectively killing live viruses.

Our Clean, Refresh and Sanitize program started with the transportation vehicle from the airport to the destination. If it was a dedicated contract company, then we made sure they agreed to adhere to our checklist to disinfect the entire vehicle interior. If it was a local airport transport company, then we ensured they could meet our guidelines for our customers.

Our customers agreed to a pre-trip protocol of temperature checks that continued daily, along with regular hand washing. At night, all common areas were sanitized, and between trips we did an even deeper cleaning, including using atomizing sprayers to ensure every crack and crevice was sanitized.

Our program was so thorough that once we submitted it to every country we operated in, not only was it accepted without change but several countries adopted it as their blueprint for reopening.

Our next challenge was what to do if a customer showed symptoms during the adventure. We outlined plans for each destination to work from, based on their weekly program and available local health care and quarantine procedures.

Unfortunately, not every destination's government had put into place solid plans for dealing with those who became ill while traveling. Once tourists started returning to these unprepared destinations, their local health care and isolation units were quickly overwhelmed. Inadequate quarantine hotels, unhealthy meal delivery options are a few examples of the problems travelers faced early on. Here, our local teams always stepped in, delivering better meals, sorting out their accommodations, and assisting local officials in getting them safely home.

In the late summer and early fall of 2020, I visited several of our destinations to check on the reopening process and see that all the guidelines we had were in place and ready for our customers to return. Despite my flying around and visiting other countries, I was never ill or symptomatic. The same was true of most of our customers. By the end of 2020, approximately 50 percent of our destinations were open and by spring of 2021, 75 percent were open. However, some destinations remained closed to tourists for two years. Once these holdouts started reopening, they realized, too late, the severe negative impact on the mental and financial health of their people and businesses. I know some will defend these extended government shutdowns, but in my opinion, the long term mental and financial toll hit harder than the virus. I hope future government leaders will work to keep their people as healthy as possible while also keeping their economic doors open.

I was extremely proud of my entire team for stepping up during what I hope was a once in a lifetime global disruption. I had asked more of my team during this time than ever before, in any of my businesses. Not one person complained about the workload. Everyone understood we were in the most disruptive business environment ever experienced and it was going to take a collective effort to emerge stronger than before.

We came up with so many remarkable Customer Engagement Initiatives during that time. I think it's safe to say that we probably would have never considered them had the pandemic not forced our hand. We've kept many of the initiatives in place to this day. The biggest take away here is that there are hundreds of ways to get you and your business through major disruptions, you just haven't thought of them yet!

RUN YOUR BUSINESS AS A BUSINESS

Every successful entrepreneur has their own unique success story. There's no one-size-fits-all formula for success, but there are some common traits among those whose businesses thrive. For instance, many entrepreneurs start small, with family and friends as their first customers. They often rely on word of mouth, at least in the beginning, to grow their business. Then, once things are up and running, they grow their business by advertising, and adding new products and/or services.

One thing common to all business owners is pride of ownership. I've met many business owners who are happy to say they succeeded because they poured their heart and soul into their business, and that no one can run it the way they do. Unfortunately, this can also be the reason why they can't grow past a certain point. Many entrepreneurs make the unfortunate mistake of making the business all about themselves. They put so much emphasis on how hard they work, how much they run the day-to-day business and how much they interact with their customers that they become synonymous with the company name. While building personal loyalty with your customers is a great way to start out, there's only so much you can do on your own. To continue to grow your business, you must enable your staff to grow into prominent customer-facing roles.

Making yourself indispensable will hurt your business growth in the long run. I have seen this in multiple scenarios when business owners ask me about how to expand, or how to attract a buyer. I always start with the question, "How many of your existing customers are only patronizing your business because of you and not only for your product or customer service?" We have all seen locally owned businesses that change ownership and then quickly decline. We have all also seen locally owned, successful businesses that branch out to a second location and the second ones grows while the first one declines. When an owner focuses all their attention on the new location without properly preparing the staff remaining in the original location, that business will slowly walk away.

Long term customers feel a certain loyalty to an owner and stay through the good times and bad. When a business owner sells, that loyalty is now voided, and the customer feels free to choose another place of business without any guilt. If your goal is to never expand to additional locations or sell the business when you retire, then by all means, stay the soul of the business and take care of your customers face-to-face.

If you want to expand your business or someday might wish to sell it for a profit, my best advice to you is to run your business like a business instead of making it all about you.

I am conscious of how my businesses operate when I'm not around. I make sure I have exceptionally trained staff who will handle my customers' needs just the same as I would. I am always happy if a customer wants to speak directly to me, but I get even more excited when I hear from a customer who reports that someone on my team took excellent care of them.

I'll bet that if you are a business owner reading this, you're probably thinking, "Yeah, but not one of my staff members will work as hard as I do or be as dedicated as I am, and it will cost me some business." This is true. When I had opened enough Taco Bell locations that I needed to add a District Manager position to help me run them while I focused on the growth aspect, I knew customer service would likely take a hit. I also knew that this would be a trade-off, at least in the short term. But I made sure to train my manager well and to circle back to the customer service aspect of the business often, with us both keeping customer service top of mind while I spent time growing the business.

Making sure your business runs smoothly even when you're not there is the best way to run a business that is scalable and sellable.

MARKET ANALYSIS, NOT MARKET PARALYSIS

What sparks a person's desire to become a scuba diver or world adventurer? And how does a traveler decide to take an Aggressor Adventures vacation? These are important questions specific to the success of my business and it's important that I know the answers to these and so many other questions.

No matter what business you're in, you must know your customer; you must know who they are, where they are from and what they like. You must also know what triggers their buying decisions. To know these details, you must collect data about your customers. I admit, I'm a data hog. I want to learn everything I can about our guests, but I avoid getting bogged down by data points. I've seen entrepreneurs get so caught up in the process of information gathering that it prevents them from taking action. They're either too busy collecting data or they're too busy interpreting it. In either case, it ends up being bad for business.

I guess my advice to you if you're looking to start a business or grow an existing business, is to absolutely do the research you'll need to do to know your market, but don't let it distract you from serving your customers.

Over the years I've been able to identify differences in our global customer base. I think they're interesting, and my fellow adventurers who read this might agree, so I've decided to share them here.

A major unifying trait amongst our guests is that they realize the comfort and convenience of the all-inclusive small group experience we provide and that it represents a cost savings over that of a typical à la cart vacation. Most will tell you they'll happily select Aggressor Adventures at a given destination, and that their only regret is they didn't discover us sooner.

Our North American guests in their late forties typically book week-long trips once a year. By their mid-fifties, we notice they tend to add on a few days to either end of their vacation for touring local cultural and historical sites. Those guests in their sixties often set aside two weeks for their vacation, and they often book more than one trip a year. This makes sense, as older guests tend to have more free time and greater financial resources to spend on travel.

North Americans typically enjoy traveling to every location around the world with us. Not just to the most well know destinations. Contrast that with our youngest set of our customers, from Asia. The Asian adventurer is typically in their late twenties to early thirties. They have an enormous sense of adventure due to in part to recent economic advances in their home countries that are making leisure travel more accessible. They rarely book more than a weeklong trip and usually want to travel to destinations where large animals, land and sea, are routinely encountered.

European travelers tend to be somewhere in the middle of the pack. They are often in their mid-thirties to mid-forties. They rarely take less than a two-week holiday and it is not unusual for a three-week vacation to be the norm. They are horrified that most North Americans only get one week of vacation a year. The European is more likely to be a step above most of the world in their travel experience having started as a young child with their family routinely visiting foreign countries. Our customers from Russia and Slavic countries are an anomaly. They are typically mid-forties to mid-sixties, and they want to see big animals, period. They have almost zero interest in nature hikes, cultural tours or small marine creatures like nudibranchs. Give them Darwin in the Galapagos Islands or Cocos Island with the massive schools of hammerheads or large Asian elephant herds in Sri Lanka and they are the happy.

Based on our market analysis, we must paint the picture of a "typical" adventurer with a broad brush. Demographics are as diverse as our worldwide destinations and that is why I love this business so much! One thing that unifies all adventurers is a passion for exploring. Getting out to as many destinations as possible, diving, site seeing and interacting with the locals while swapping stories with other passionate travelers fills my adventurous spirit every time.

START WITH A VISION.
EXECUTE WITH A STRATEGY.

Branding, marketing, and advertising. All three overlap but each element is extremely important to successful business promotion. I know there are a lot of resources where you can find this information, but I felt it's important enough to include here, if nothing more than to share my experience with what works for my business.

I view my logo as the main ingredient in branding. A logo must be visually appealing, with a simple, clean look that represents your business and will help distinguish it from others. The design must be versatile and scalable, so it reproduces well on smaller items like business cards, t-shirts and hats, to larger items like cars, boats and billboards. A logo needs to look appealing when printed in a single color and in full color. And when reproduced in embroidery, too. If you intend to use your logo on embroidered items like polo shirts, hats and tote bags, for example, it's important. Many logo designers go off the deep end when designing logos that are too detailed. They might look great on a computer screen, but they look terrible in print or when embroidered on a garment.

When working with a graphic designer it's good to start by providing examples of colors, fonts and basic designs you like. This will help get the logo design process going. Be sure to ask the designer to provide mock-ups of how your potential logo will look when printed and embroidered. Recent advancements in AI make this process simple, fast, and economical. Don't be afraid to ask for design revisions. Logo design is important to your overall branding and marketing goals, so it's important to settle on a design you like and will meet your business's needs.

One final note on branding is that over time, your logo might need a refresh. It might be that your business changed in ways that call for a new look, or maybe it's just that your logo design didn't stand the test of time. In either case, consider this a good thing because it means you've succeeded at longevity. Rebranding requires another investment of time and money, but change is inevitable, so get used to it.

This brings me to marketing and advertising. The goal is to deliver your brand's message to potential customers in a way that makes them remember you and want to do business with you.

I challenge my graphic design team to create ad campaigns that utilize our logo and core marketing message in a way that excites our customers and invites them to join us on an adventure. This is one area of my business that I routinely push back on during the creative process. I scrutinize every image, every text block, every graphic. If it appears an ad campaign is missing the mark, I insist that changes be made. Most of the time we'll accomplish this with one or two revisions, although there have been times when I've scrapped ideas, and we started over. At the end of the day, it is my company, and I am the one who will be criticized, not the agency that created the ad. Take the time, every time, to get it right.

Advertising is all about putting your brand's message where it will reach the most potential customers. Two big questions you must consider are: 1) how and where do I position my advertising? And 2) how do I allocate my budget?

First off, it's important that you know as much as possible about who your customers are, so you can position ads that reach them with your marketing message. In my case, advertising scuba diving adventures in publications dedicated to scuba diving is a perfect fit. That's easy. But what about advertising Aggressor Adventures Safaris or River Cruises in a diving magazine? Will divers want to spend their time and money on a non-diving trip? Practically every ad exec you ask will tell you no, that it'd be a waste of money because the return is simply not there. And they might be right. But it's up to me to decide. Adventurous divers know my brand's history of providing excellent customer service, so maybe if they see an adventure travel ad in a scuba magazine, they'll book a safari or river cruise with us.

It never hurts to test new markets. Soon enough you'll know if it's working or not. Just make sure you keep track of your advertising experiments and don't pour so much of your budget into test markets that it dilutes the message you must deliver to your core customer base.

When it comes to allocating an advertising budget, I always invest in good market penetration over time. I ensure my company's message is compelling and consistent, and I make each ad a fresh message instead of running the same ad over and over. It's a matter of relevance. Staying in front of my customers with attractive branding and an exciting marketing message ensures I get the most out of my advertising budget over time. This strategy, combined with our standard of providing excellent customer service, helps Aggressor Adventures receive a lot of word-of-mouth advertising, too. And having happy customers sell your services for you is the ultimate reward.

HOW AN AGGRESSOR ADVENTURES DESTINATION HAPPENS

I get asked a lot how I develop and finalize new Aggressor Adventures destinations around the world. With multiple languages, local regulations and time zones, it is an adventure in itself!

I have a long list of new destinations that I am always chipping away at. There are several factors that we consider before greenlighting a new Aggressor destination. First of course is always the ability of the destination to deliver an amazing adventure for at least a week at a time. Between myself and my operations team, one of us will travel to an area that we believe may be an exciting addition to the company. While there we map out possible itineraries that our future guests will likely enjoy. We also spend time photographing and videoing the local attractions, touring hotels and resorts, learning about the local culture and history. We make sure the destination has adequate support facilities, qualified tradespeople, and reliable suppliers of high-quality provisions and other supplies. We also setup appointments with officials to work on the necessary permits and licenses.

One important consideration is that we can cultivate a solid working relationship with local government and private sector shareholders at a destination. In most instances, our business investment is warmly welcomed, as it creates new local jobs and brings money to the local economy, but there have been times when our best efforts are not met with enthusiasm. For instance, one time we faced significant challenges getting parts cleared through customs. It was suggested that the process might move quickly if we "greased the wheels" so to speak, but we never go down that road. Sadly, we couldn't gain local support of our program. We pulled out of that destination when it became clear we couldn't guarantee the high level of service our customers expect from Aggressor Adventures.

Since all our adventures require air travel to reach the destination, airlines also play a large role in our final decision. Our market research includes determining how many major airlines regularly service the destination and how much flights typically cost. With regional carriers, we must research their operational histories and make sure they are reputable and certified by numerous aviation authorities.

Even after all this lengthy fact-finding process is accomplished, the next step is to find a suitable investor or investors who will become the local Licensee. They must prove their willingness and ability to deliver the Aggressor Adventures our guests expect. There are times when I have a potential destination that sits dormant for years after we've greenlighted it as a suitable location simply because we're still waiting to find a Licensee that shares our values and vision.

Sometimes, a new owner comes to us and sometimes we network until we find one. I always start with a video call to meet them and gauge their interest, enthusiasm and ability to financially support the operation. It might surprise you to learn that about 1 in 10 potential candidates make it past this first step. I arrange an in-person meeting for those that pass the initial interview. This is always the most important step in my making the final decision.

During this meeting I review with them numerous scenarios of things that could go wrong during an adventure and ask them to describe how would they address the issue and make it right for our customers. In many instances, the potential new owner has experience in the service industry and especially with adventure travel, but this isn't always the case. Some new Licensees come from other industries. This has proven beneficial, as their fresh perspective offers us the chance to explore new ways to enhance and strengthen our brands.

Once the lengthy approval process is completed, the next objective is to review the calendar for launching new destinations. We can stagger them to offer each new destination to be featured as a star attraction in the Aggressor Adventures lineup of destinations.

But wait; there's more. Before the first guests can arrive, the approval of the resort or yacht and staff selection/training must take place. Our Operations department works hands-on with the new Licensees to ensure they and their staff understand and can fully implement the program while strictly adhering to our SOPs. While this is happening at the destination, back in Augusta, GA, the IT department is programming the new destination into our reservations system; the marketing team is developing advertising materials that can be translated into several languages, and is scheduling releases in magazines and on various travel websites; and the Boutique team is busy cranking out logo items including staff uniforms and retail products that will be shipped to the destination.

If this seems like a lot, it is! There are so many moving parts to an Aggressor Adventures destination. And every part must fit into place with careful attention to detail, and with the precision of a finely crafted Swiss timepiece. I'm proud to say that everyone on all our teams loves the challenge. We're always jazzed about creating new adventures for Aggressor Adventures customers.

BUILDING THE ULTIMATE LIVEABOARD

As I mentioned in a previous essay, the original Aggressor Fleet consisted of commercial oil rig crew transport vessels that Aggressor founder Paul Haines converted into liveaboard dive yachts. I admire his ingenuity, repurposing his existing fleet and transform the former crew boats into luxurious yachts for divers, but ever since I purchased Aggressor Fleet in 2007, I had dreamed of designing and building the next generation of diving liveaboard. I'd kept a file of notes that included many ideas and suggestions from our guests. This time, I wouldn't be refitting an existing vessel but would be a yacht specifically designed and built for divers. I'd have a clean slate.

In 2018 my dream started to take shape as I started construction of the new *Cayman Aggressor*. My list of must-haves was long: in addition to having a spacious dive deck with an ample entry/exit area and individual storage areas for divers' gear and cameras; a spacious interior lounge with dining room seating at two large tables so our guests could socialize during meals; comfortable shaded and open outdoor lounge areas; and of course, the guest suites would feature premium bedding and include ensuite bathrooms. Natural light was also high on my list, so we designed the dining area with floor to ceiling windows.

The designing and engineering proved to be a significant challenge, but I didn't impose a firm deadline for completion, so work crews weren't under pressure to cut corners just to meet a splash date.

We had huge lists of every item needed to build and outfit a luxury liveaboard yacht. Every detail was recorded on spreadsheets. Lots of spreadsheets. In the spreadsheets, I included links to each website used to source parts and supplies, so we could easily place re-orders if needed.

As the construction began, we made multiple trips to Panama to check on the progress. I did end up making a few tough decisions to tear out and reconstruct some deck surfaces and framing we weren't satisfied with, which set our completion date back several months. But I knew it would be worth it.

Once the build was done, we started weeks of sea trials to ensure all the yacht's onboard systems were dialed in and the vessel was ready to begin work. Once it reached the Cayman Islands, we ran a gauntlet of local inspections, fire and safety drills before we were issued our certifications and operating permits. While this was happening, the staff were busy readying the interior, including stocking the galley, making beds and detailing every inch of the yacht.

When the day finally arrived that we transitioned from the *Cayman Aggressor IV* to the inaugural charter on the *Cayman Aggressor V*, our staff was amazing. We finished a charter on *Cayman Aggressor IV* in the morning and welcomed guests aboard the new *Cayman Aggressor V* before sunset on the same day.

You can't expect to launch a project of this magnitude without something going wrong. I was pleasantly surprised when no big problems arose that affected our Eat, Sleep & Dive® motto! We did find that the dining area, with its floor to ceiling windows, got too warm in late afternoons, even with the additional air conditioning we'd added when designing it. Applying window tinting fixed this issue without affecting the great views.

Building the *Cayman Aggressor V* was truly a dream come true. I'm proud of the design and engineering team, our Aggressor Adventures team, and of course, our onboard staff. (And I'd like to believe Paul Haines would be pleased with how far we've come since he first refit C/*Aggressor*.) We've built a yacht our guests will enjoy for many years to come.

TRUTHFULNESS & INTEGRITY

You can question every business decision I make, but never doubt my integrity. If you do, you're out the door. And you're never coming back in.

SELLING YOURSELF

Whatever business you are in, always remember that no matter how good your product or service is, you will be more successful if you are likable.

You should think about your conversations with buyers, customers or supervisors as an interview. I do a lot of radio and TV interviews and I always keep in mind that I am selling myself as much as my company and my adventures. I invite the interviewer to ask any question they want, even though they usually ask me to provide them with pre-written questions. The more seasoned interviewers will be able to roll with impromptu questions depending on my answers. This allows for more of a conversational interview that has an organic flow rather than feeling highly scripted.

Any time you're being interviewed, you must be quick-thinking and always craft an answer that will help you sell your product or service. If possible, start out using a personal story that ties into the answer. This gives the people watching or listening to the interview the chance to get to learn more about you and maybe feel a personal connection to you and your business.

About half the TV interviews I do are taped, so producers can edit out small gaffs before the program airs. Still, I like to pretend we're on live, and I strive to make every answer factual, credible, and interesting on the first try. I have yet to need a second take on any answers. This might sound difficult, but it will come naturally if you're an expert on your product or service.

When you are grooming employees to take on more customer-facing rolls, never let them get in front of an interviewer until you are 100 percent certain it will come off as a successful sell, both for your company and them. Letting someone "get their feet wet" in front of an interviewer will

Wayne B. Brown

not only be a failure for your company, but the interviewer will also look bad and probably never ask to highlight your company again.

I am frequently asked to speak impromptu when attending at socials or informal gatherings. I am always happy to speak about my company. I keep in mind that I am also selling myself, not in an egocentric way but as an ethical, honest, hardworking person. This is where the integrity of what I am telling them comes through.

140

KEEPING THE EGO ON THE GROUND

Growing my Taco Bell franchise territory meant I needed to spend more time traveling. I also had to be more mindful of my time, so I started chartering a turboprop airplane from a local charter company. Chartering a private plane was saving me two days of time spent traveling on commercial flights, and it usually meant I didn't have to stay in a hotel overnight. If I planned my schedule carefully, I could leave early in the morning and fly to one of the farthest cities and spend the day touring my stores, meeting with the staff and scouting potential sites for future Taco Bell locations, and still return home that evening.

As I continued to grow my business and add more Taco Bell locations across the southeastern United States, I was chartering the turboprop often. It wasn't long before my business reached a tipping point, where investing in my own plane would be less expensive than chartering. This was a huge step, one that I weighed carefully. I've seen more than a few entrepreneurs let their egos override their business sense when making this kind of decision. I was determined not to let that happen to me. If owning a plane made solid financial sense, fine. I vowed to never let myself get personally attached to any business asset, no matter what. This mindset is essential to surviving changes in business.

I found a good deal on a used Beechcraft KingAir B200. Its low operational and maintenance cost earned the KingAir a reputation as a workhorse of private aviation. For flights of less than 1,500 miles per day it only required one pilot, which represented a savings on crew costs. Depending on the configuration, the KingAir accommodates six to 10 passengers with plenty of cargo space, so longer flights would be no problem, provided you make fuel stops and plan for possibly overnighting. It was this KingAir that I took to the Galápagos Islands on that fateful *Galapagos Aggressor* charter that started me down the Aggressor Adventures road.

The downside of this aircraft is its ceiling, or maximum altitude limit of 25,000 feet. It does not allow you to climb high enough to get above bad weather, so you end up with bumpy, sometimes very bumpy rides, especially in the south, where mid-summer afternoon thunderstorms are common.

Fortunately, as my restaurant and real estate investments grew, I was able to upgrade to a light jet that would solve the altitude constraint. I ended up with a Beechjet 400A. It could get to altitude quickly, fly faster and farther and was within the budget I had set for a light jet. It was more expensive to operate because it required two pilots for every flight and came with greater fuel and maintenance costs. Still, I managed to stay within my new, increased budget.

Once I was negotiating the purchase of Aggressor, I was looking for an aircraft that could get me to as many of the Aggressor destinations as possible. The Beechjet was not going to make long overwater flights, even from the mainland USA to Hawaii, which is the range test for getting around the world. Another budget increase allowed for a larger jet that could get from mainland USA to Hawaii and from there to any country in the world. If I was going to make this leap to save time flying commercial aircraft, I needed a fast jet. At that time, the fastest private aircraft was the Citation X. It could fly at Mach.92 and at an altitude of 47,000 feet. Most commercial aircraft fly at 35,000 feet so we would be way above them and would not have to compete with their airspace.

I set the annual budget for a Citation X and found a slightly used one at a great price, 12 million. I also remained solid in my commitment to only using the jet as a "no ego" business asset. But this doesn't mean I didn't allow myself to enjoy the perks of owning the Citation. It was a beauty with massive engines, a stand-up cabin, 8 lay-flat seats, a large bathroom, a full galley, and modern avionics that my pilots loved. I once returned from a meeting in Orange County, California to Augusta in three hours and 20 minutes. It was crazy fast, quiet, and comfortable. The longest trip I took was a tour of several Aggressor destinations in the Pacific and then to Australia to check on potential business there. The trip included a stop in the Marshall Islands to refuel. The island was not much wider than the runway, with beautiful clear water on each side with fringing reefs.

While the flight crew tending to the refueling, I quickly put on some swim shorts, grabbed my mask and fins and went for a swim. The reefs were extremely healthy and covered in colorful marine life. I remember feeling a deep sense of satisfaction, looking up from the reef to see my plane in the distance.

This was in early 2007. The happy memory has stayed with me to this day, but unfortunately, everything was about to change. By mid-summer, aviation fuel costs had doubled, and it was quickly eating through my annual budget. I had to make the tough call to put the jet on the market. Typically, larger private aircraft are sold at the end of a year when people are taking advantage of tax breaks, so in December 2007 I sold the Citation X for a small profit. This turned out to be an extremely timely decision! If you were working or in business in 2008, you will remember what is now referred to as the 2007-2008 Global Financial Crisis. It is considered the most severe worldwide economic crisis since the Great Depression. One of the hardest-hit areas was private aviation, since a private jet is a luxury, not a necessity. By the end of 2008, the same Citation X I sold for a profit a year earlier was listed for four million dollars less than I sold it for. I was so glad I stuck to my commitment not to let my emotions interfere with financial decisions. If I had chosen ego over integrity, it would have been an expensive lesson.

HONESTY AS AN ANTIDOTE TO NONSENSE

When it comes to the people I aim to associate with, integrity is a fundamental component of the relationship. To me, the word integrity describes iron-clad honesty, the no-nonsense kind that doesn't waiver, no matter what. It's about doing the right thing, without any drama.

Some years ago, I owned a business in partnership with a couple friends. We decided to sell the business, and during our first discussion about selling, I said, "I know money has a way of making enemies out of friends. I want to make sure right from the start, that we go through the financials carefully and put everything on the table, and we determine ahead of time how the proceeds will be divided. We need to avoid a situation that could impact our friendship." We all agreed, and we enlisted a broker to handle the sale.

We each submitted our financial records, which showed I had invested the most money in our venture. The broker used the financial data to come up with the amount each partner was to receive at closing. Because I'd put in the most money, I'd earn the most from the sale.

The math was simple, but it didn't stop the situation from getting complicated because one of the partners insisted on receiving a larger share. This might be okay when you split a lunch tab and one person's burger is more expensive than another's salad; maybe you're only talking a few dollars' difference, so it's no big deal. You're friends, right? But when selling a business that's got a hefty price tag attached and one partner has put in more money than the other, "Let's just split it" doesn't cut it. Both the broker and I tried explaining the numbers to him, but he dug in, insisting I forfeit a portion of my share "to make it even." It ended the relationship.

Our wives were friends. My former partner's wife confided to my wife Dana, "Well, he gets dug in like this sometimes, but eventually he gets over it." Dana knows this isn't how I operate, and aptly said, "Not Wayne. Wayne doesn't get over it. Once you're out, you're out."

I feel proud that the people I welcome into my inner circle are the ones I know I can trust. I think this is because over the years, I have developed what I refer to as a highly reliable bullshit detector. I typically know right away when someone is trying to feed me a line of BS.

I love the line from the movie, *As Good as It Gets*, in which Jack Nicholson's character answers his apartment door to deal with a whacky neighbor. He says, "Sell crazy someplace else. We're all stocked up here." The film, which came out in late 1997, earned Nicholson an Academy Award for Best Actor.

I think the reason the "sell crazy someplace else" line resonates with me is that just like Nicholson's character, I'm not interested in drama. Sure, every person will have their share of crazy stuff to deal with in life, but I think some people go looking for crazy-making situations.

I once heard somebody say with exasperation, "If you don't have sense enough to come in out of the rain, you're gonna get wet." Some people seem to stand in the rain just so they can complain about being wet. Not me. If I'm gonna get wet, I'd rather be out enjoying a scuba dive than dealing with drama.

WHAT KEEPS ME UP AT NIGHT

An interviewer once asked me, "What is it that keeps you up at night, anything?" I usually sleep well at night, but I understood the question. If there's anything I'd lose sleep over, it's my concern that we're not delivering on a promise.

Aggressor Adventures sells adventure travel that focuses on luxury travel. But we're more than a travel company. We're in the "dreams come true" business. We sell customer satisfaction by providing the very best service we can offer. I'm talking five stars. Or better.

There are countless variables that affect the overall outcome of one of our adventures. For instance, we can't control the weather or what the divers will see underwater, or if they can check all Big Five animal sightings on a Sri Lankan safari. But there's so much we can do to ensure they enjoy the experience, including the accommodations and meals and guest services, and more.

I want to ensure that our guests are wowed, and they end a trip with us feeling like their adventure was better than they could ever have imagined. This is particularly challenging, since we operate all over the world, with varying cultural norms. What one culture in one part of the world thinks is five-star service might be what another considers two-star. I get concerned about our goal to deliver our own Aggressor Adventures standard of five-star service in every location around the world. The truth is, this is what I would lose sleep over, and it's what I think about every waking hour. Are we delivering the best? And how can we make it even better?

THE LONG GAME

My good friend Frank is a very successful insurance agent. Any time the topic of business comes up, I'm guaranteed to hear him say, "It's all about the revenue." He's right. Every business lives or dies by the amount of revenue it generates. The goal is to always make more than you spend, right? Well, yes and no. Every business that succeeds over time must play the long game when analyzing risk versus reward. By this I mean there are times when you have to spend to earn.

Investing and continually reinvesting in the growth of your business is paramount to its long-term success. I learned this during my Taco Bells days, and it's the same with Aggressor Adventures. I'm talking about investing capital in expanding to new locations and investing capital in making regular repairs and upgrades to existing locations. The businesses that just take money from the till and never spend anything on upkeep are the businesses that die from neglect. If I still had the same barebones liveaboard boats that Aggressor Fleet operated in 1984, there would be no Aggressor Adventures around today to be writing about. Without spending capital to improve the flagship *Cayman Aggressor* boat and eventually replacing it with one that's bigger and better, we'd have fallen behind the market instead of maintaining our place as the leader in the industry.

I have a different perspective on "it's all about the revenue" as it applies to discounts and special offers, too. Some business experts caution against lowering prices to increase sales. Is this a bad thing? Here's my yes/no viewpoint. Of course we can't afford to give away our adventures, but I know my fixed costs and my profit margin. I know I can strategically offer specials to fill charters during off-peak travel periods, for instance. Every dollar above my fixed cost goes straight to the bottom line. I also know that some customers will only book when a price is discounted, so I want to cast as wide a net as possible to catch every potential guest. I would never want to exclude this subset, because their business adds up over time and contributes to our profitability.

Does every Adventure *have* to be profitable? Here we go with the long game again. On rare occasions a particular booking is light, but I don't rush to cancel an adventure because we have too few guests for that trip. We have run a few adventures at break-even, or even at a slight loss. It's part of doing business. When our guests on the low-volume adventure get an even better experience due to the higher staff-to-guest ratio, they're more likely to book with us again, and they're likely to boast about Aggressor Adventures to their friends. This kind of marketing is priceless, and it sure as hell beats canceling their trip and alienating them from doing future business with us.

Here's more insight into customer service. Things will go wrong with customer service in every business. This is a fact, no matter how hard you try. It is how you handle it that impacts future revenue. If one of my guests did not get the full experience we offer, and they paid for, due to a failure on our part, they deserve to be compensated for that. I know you are probably thinking, "Yeah, but what about the people who just can't be satisfied and will always complain, no matter what?" Honestly, those perpetually cranky peoples represent a very small percentage of the customer base of any business. When I receive a legitimate complaint that outlines how we failed to deliver on our promise, I use as much data as I can to calculate what a guest missed out on so I can fully explain my logic and back it up with numbers. Then I offer fair compensation. Because it's the right thing to do. Integrity is key. And I can tell you from experience, it's a good investment in the good name of my brand. This is one of the most important lessons I make sure every potential Aggressor Adventures Licensee understands before making the yes/no decision to offer them a license. If we fail, we fix it.

And that's final. If a new licensee isn't on board with this forthright and honest way of doing business, it can hurt the brand. And we can't afford that. So, back to, "It's all about the revenue." I wish it was that simple, but it's complicated.

THE TRUTH ABOUT FAILURE

I wrote about eliminating the fear of failure in a previous essay, but I want to mention it again here because I truly consider failure a positive rather than a negative. Thinking about potential failure is a way to rule out what might not work while you're looking to find what does work. When I'm thinking of new ideas to implement for the business, I might make a list of 10 possible new ideas. Next, I'd think of all the ways in which each idea might fail and start crossing them off the list. In the end, maybe I've got one or two ideas remaining that might be worth trying.

Let's say I implement an idea and it fails. Maybe the idea is still valid, but I need to tweak it to get it to work. Maybe not. Maybe it's just not viable and I need to move on to the next idea. The point is that I can always take something positive away from the experience and learn from it.

If you need a hit of inspiration, Google, "list of people whose businesses initially failed and later succeeded." A quick Internet search will provide names including Bill Gates, Walt Disney, Steve Jobs and Oprah Winfrey. Ray Croc was rejected by more than 200 restaurants before he sold his McDonald's franchise concept. Thomas Edison failed thousands of times before perfecting the incandescent light bulb.

———————

I have a silly story to share about failure. We bought some property about 30 miles outside of Augusta, GA. It's in a rural area that was once part of a 500-acre plantation once belonging to a Revolutionary War soldier. His great grandson still lives there. He's up in years now, but he's a nice guy and he's quite a storyteller who knows a lot about the Revolutionary War. In fact, he gave me a book about it.

Anyway, he likes telling stories about "back in the day." He told me that when he was a young boy, the nearest school was more than 20 miles away. Kids would either walk or ride horses to get there and they'd stay all week, camping out on the school grounds before making the 20-mile trek home on weekends. As the story goes, there was this one kid who, after a rainstorm, showed up to school a day late. When the teacher asked him why he was late, he explained, "Teacher, it was so muddy, every time I'd take one step forward, I'd slide two steps backward." When the teacher tried scolding him, asking, "Well then, if this is true, how did you finally make it here?" To this, he replied, "I walked backward."

I know. I told you this is a silly story. But it made me laugh, especially because the old guy laughed so hard after telling it. But then I thought, you know what? Sometimes this is the way things work. If you are failing in a one step forward, two steps backward way, stop. If you literally turn around—try something different—you might make forward progress!

BULLSHIT

Whenever I meet new people, whether personal or business,
I always have my bullshit meter fully charged. Surround yourself with people
you can trust and don't waste a minute on those you can't trust.

WE'RE GOING THERE

Why would my book about entrepreneurship and success in business and in life include a section on bullshit? Because a lot of people exaggerate, and some people outright lie. It's important to recognize this fact, and I can't come up with a word that does a better job of defining egregious, outright lies than "bullshit." As business leaders and entrepreneurs, we must fine-tune our bullshit detectors and not be afraid to call BS when we see it. Most importantly, we must not buy into lies and let them distract us from our goals.

ON ENTITLEMENT

I recently saw a social media post in which a guy boasts that he finally got the position he deserves. His comment struck a nerve. As a kid, I learned at an early age that if I wanted something, I needed to go after it, to earn it. I don't recall any of my friends ever using the term, "deserve." We all knew how to hustle, doing odd jobs for a few bucks when we wanted spending money.

A mindset of entitlement is a slippery slope. If you're not careful, instead of being self-motivated to achieve success through hard work, you might find yourself slacking off and then blaming others when you don't get what you want. Having something handed to you doesn't feel anywhere near as satisfying as holding it in your hands after you've worked hard to earn it.

WHAT DO YOU MEAN, "NO PANCAKES?"

A couple days before we left Germany, we moved out of our apartment and stayed at the hotel on base. We slept in the first morning, having been tired from finishing packing our household goods and arranging for everything to be shipped back to Florida. Anyway, we arrived at the hotel restaurant ready to enjoy a leisurely breakfast. It was 9:50 am. The sign posted on the wall above the menu indicated breakfast was served until 10 am. Like many toddlers, Justin's favorite breakfast was pancakes. When I placed the order, the cook said, "No pancakes." She motioned to the griddle and said she'd just finished cleaning it, so he'd need to have something else.

We were the only ones in the place and my kid wanted pancakes for breakfast. At a restaurant that was supposed to serve breakfast until 10 am. This is the kind of customer service failure that has gotten to me my entire life. It's not how you treat customers. So, I called BS and stood my ground. I politely but firmly insisted on getting Justin his pancakes. She fussed a little but finally relented and made the pancakes. Everything was fine.

I share this story because this pancake situation underscored why my leaving the military was a good decision. In the military, pushing back against poor service just wasn't done. Granted, this was a civilian-run restaurant on base, but I think you can understand my point.

Customer service is about serving customers. Most of the time it's simply a matter of doing the thing you say you will do. Not doing it, especially when you have all the tools or materials or ingredients you need to get the job done sitting right in front of you? That's bullshit.

THE BULLSHIT DETECTOR

I regularly get calls from travel journalists asking to interview me for some travel piece they are writing. A guy recently reached out because he was writing an article about people who own adventure travel businesses, so the questions were more about me than about travel. He asked a question about licensing, wanting me to explain how, with all the different cultures and personalities around the world, I determine which potential Licensee gets awarded an Aggressor Adventures license. That was an easy question. I told him it all boiled down to my superior bullshit detector.

I was recently in an Asian country meeting with a potential new Licensee of my brand. He is originally from Europe but has lived in the South Pacific for over 20 years. When in these meetings I am always on the alert for not only their business background but also integrity, sincerity and truthfulness. I want them to also be looking for those same qualities in me. During our initial meeting, my bullshit detector's needle never left full green. That is always a great start!

One of the ways I check for truthfulness is by creating a hypothetical customer service scenario that I feel certain they cannot fully deliver. I'll ask, "What if I want 'x, y and z' for the guests? Can you provide it?" If they're too quick to say "yes" it'll push my BS detector's needle into the red. I'm okay if they ponder the question and maybe propose alternatives, or maybe if they give me a partial "yes" but with some limits. That said, what I'm really looking for is a solid "no" answer.

Why? It's simple. I have built my brand reputation on honesty. Our goal is always to provide the highest possible level of customer service to our guests. To achieve this goal, we must be honest with our customers about what we can and cannot deliver. Our licensees must uphold this business philosophy. I have no problem calling a disappointed guest if we failed to deliver on our brand promises, because no matter how hard we try, there will always be instances when circumstances beyond our control lead to a less-than-perfect outcome. But if I'm put in a situation where I have to call a disappointed guest and explain why they were promised something that wasn't possible? That's a whole 'nother story. An honest failure is an honest failure. But failing because we promised something we knew we couldn't deliver? That's bullshit. It's called lying. And it's unacceptable.

NO SPECIAL DEALS

I do not negotiate the terms of a Licensing Agreement. Every Licensee gets the same deal. If you ever negotiate your terms with even one Licensee, you'll have them all wondering if someone else is getting a better deal. It's important to keep the playing field level for all.

The same goes for the thousands of reselling travel agencies around the world that book travel with Aggressor Adventures. Every year I get a few travel specialists that demand a bigger piece of the commission pie, insisting that if they do not get a heftier commission, they will stop selling my brand. The quick and easy answer is no. If I give one reseller, no matter how much of my annual sales they represent, even one percent more, that opens the door for them to suspect, rightfully, that I'm not true to my word and it'll have them wondering if other resellers are getting an even better deal.

Your business boundaries won't mean anything if you don't uphold them. There's a saying in the south, "Good fences make good neighbors." It's true. The respect you will gain, even from those that initially scoff at your hardcore stance, will help your business stakeholders know where the fences are.

SELLING SNAKE OIL

I can't tell you how many times I've heard investment pitches advertising a "turnkey" business, describing it as some kind of magical business that just runs itself and makes you tons of money without it ever taking any of your time running it. You just show up to collect the cash, is all. This is total bullshit. There is no such thing as a turnkey business. Whoever came up with that term is selling snake oil. If you want to be a successful entrepreneur, rest assured you'll need to do the work.

FRANCHISE FRUSTRATIONS

There was a time when I felt frustrated by how slowly the Taco Bell Franchise Board was communicating information to its franchisees. I wanted regular updates on things like proposed menu changes and marketing plans, but they weren't coming fast enough. My frustration prompted me to seek a position on the board. It's a two-year commitment, but I felt ready for it, so I wrote a letter to each franchisee in the southeast territory explaining my decision to run for the board. I never brought up my concerns about the current board member who represented our region. I simply laid out my vision for improvements. I followed up with a phone call asking other franchise owners where they thought I should focus my attention if elected to the board.

I won the board position. After each board meeting, I mailed each franchisee in my territory a thick stack of notes, which included a summary sheet on top. I made good on my promise to keep everyone informed.

I was put on the Operations committee and the Technology committee. These two areas were right up my alley. The operations committee covered new equipment, architecture and design, and training/restaurant operations. The Technology committee covered all the computer systems and point-of-sale systems that were already in place as well as planning for the future. This is where I'll share a prime example of where large companies can start to stumble and fail.

At the time, Taco Bell was owned by PepsiCo along with KFC and Pizza Hut. PepsiCo wanted to spin off these three brands into their owned company which was named Tricon (Three Icons). The new Tricon now owed PepsiCo 4 billion dollars. To help repay this, Taco Bell, which at the time was 80 percent company-owned and 20 percent franchise-owned, decided to flip those numbers and sell off 60 percent of the stores to franchisees.

169

I was lucky enough to win the bidding process for all the Taco Bells in the cities of Biloxi, MS, Mobile, AL and Pensacola, FL—a total of 23 stores. I wanted to be sure the new store managers and staff knew they had someone behind them that cared and would support them to ensure every location could be successful. Every piece of broken equipment was immediately repaired or replaced. Every store had access to new clean uniforms and my District Managers' workload was reduced from 10 stores to seven, to give them time to manage well rather than just run around from store to store, putting out fires. We made salary increases and offered incentives to ensure we could keep our best and brightest leaders.

I set new, stricter guidelines on jewelry, dress and grooming. I allowed one set of earrings, one necklace and one bracelet. Facial piercings were forbidden, and men were required to be clean shaven. I know this may seem old school and outdated, but it was my business and I set high standards. Applicants were free to decide if they wanted to be part of a clean, well-run workplace. If not, they could find work someplace else.

The next year I succeeded in purchasing the Jacksonville, FL market and surrounding cities and I made the same changes and upgrades.

Now in my second year on the franchise board, I was made chairman of the Operations Committee and the Technology Committee. This more than doubled my workload for the board but I was happy to serve. Tricon had been working on developing its own point-of-sale software system and this was the year they were going to put it into overdrive.

Some large corporations get into a rut thinking they can just throw money at an idea and presto, it is a game changer. Often the only game changer in these scenarios is the amount of money that gets wasted. In this case, they started out with a director who became overwhelmed with the project. They quickly realized this and hired a veteran IT project director, Purvish Kothari. Purvish and I hit it off from day one. We shared the vision of how this project could be a win-win for every store under the Tricon brand.

The initial project director started off on the wrong foot and was trying to tackle too much in the 1.0 version of the software, a very common mistake for project rookies. Purvish and I cut down the 1.0 requirements to something that was manageable, executable and would prove the viability of our own point-of-sale software. Unfortunately, those at the top of Tricon, who were inhaling their own exhaust and thought they were infallible, were only interested in a system that could handle all three brands' menus at once and included outrageous processes like currency conversions for any country in the world where a Tricon restaurant operated. They wanted a system that could run before it could walk.

Purvish tried to explain to Tricon execs why their demands were impossible. Sadly, they persisted. Purvish knew the project would fail, so he resigned. I understood and supported his decision. This meant I was now stuck with his replacement, who Tricon decided should be from the operational side of the business, not from the tech development world. Just when you thought things could not get worse! By the end of that year, after spending 65 million dollars, they had nothing to show for it. Not even a beta test. The whole thing was bullshit.

At this point I recommended to the Franchise board that we pursue a contract with a true software company to write our own point-of-sale and not purchase the Tricon system (if it ever came to market). When I sold my Taco Bells in late 2006, there was still not a working system.

BALANCING ACT

The topic of work/life balance has been in the news a lot, especially since the events of 2020 forced the world to implement remote work strategies. There are plenty of studies, books and courses on what work/life balance is and how to achieve it. And apparently a lot of people feel stress over not having, or seeking, this balance.

Honestly, I don't get what all the fuss is about. Some experts suggest compartmentalizing your work, separating it from other components of your life. For me and a lot of my very successful, very happy friends, it's all in one big bucket! If you are enjoying what you do for a living and you love the people in your life, things balance out. You'll naturally have the motivation you need to be happy at home and productive in business.

I usually get up very early (I am writing this at 4:30 am) and start my day by responding to text messages that came in while I was asleep. There'll always be several, since my business operates 24/7. Next, I move on to emails and finally, the latest news. Working from home while I enjoy my coffee during a quiet morning is ideal. The house is quiet. With no distractions, I have time to think before banging out responses to emails. Being able to get this important work accomplished before I'm even out the door to the office helps me feel energized and ready to face the day.

I didn't grow up surrounded by extended family, so I'm not sure how having my family around me became an important life goal. I feel fortunate that Dana and I have our kids and grandchildren close by. Just last night one of the grandkids came over to have dinner with us and play some video games. When he asked me to play, I quickly finished up what I was working on so we could enjoy our time together. This is my life/work balance heaven.

HR BS

always aim to make myself available for interviews, especially from students. During an interview with a business major from a very prestigious university, the student asked me to explain how my company's Human Resource Department operates. I replied by saying, "I can summarize it in two sentences. One, I don't have a Human Resources (HR) Department. Two, I think having an HR department is the biggest waste of money a company can spend."

I was met with complete silence.

After a couple of quiet moments, he finally said, "I can't go back to my professor with that." I offered to explain my disdain for HR departments, adding that I could back it up with facts. Here goes:

Reason one. When I worked in the corporate world and had an underperforming staff member that needed to be replaced, it was always a huge struggle to fire the employee, no matter how poorly they performed or what company policies they had violated. Having to retain a poor performer, no matter how low a rung they occupy on the corporate ladder, brings the entire operation down. It's important to be able to replace them with those who can get the job done.

Reason two. Somehow, the HR department creeps like an invasive weed into other parts of the company. Before long, the HR department starts running the show. This hamstrings the entire company and prevents it from meeting important sales goals and profitability targets.

When I share this viewpoint with friends who work for or own large companies with an HR department, they are often stunned, but nod their heads in silent agreement. Some admitted they never realized the power the HR department had acquired. Still others knew but were unable, ironically due to the HR department polices, to make any changes.

175

———

My interviewer listened intently as I called bullshit on HR departments, then briefly paused before asking how I handled two personnel issues, workplace complaints and performance reviews, which are usually addressed by HR staff. Here's how that went:

Workplace complaints. People are people, so there will inevitably be personality differences amongst employees. If a conflict arises, my staff knows they can come to me, and I will listen to their complaint. I explain to my employees that my policy is straightforward; tell me who you're having the problem with, explain what is happening, and I will work to fix it. I also caution them by saying, "I don't do 'bitching' so don't come into my office wanting to complain about someone without telling me their name, because that's just a waste of time and it doesn't solve anything. I'm here for solutions."

As you can imagine, he was shocked that I would manage conflicts so bluntly. I think he was surprised to learn that this matter-of-fact approach gets problems solved. And quickly.

Annual or quarterly performance reviews. I explained that I don't fault any company that conducts reviews, but it's just not me. It's not how I operate. During my time in the military, I wrote a lot of reviews. It took up a lot of my time and I never saw any meaningful change come out of the process.

Once again, my policy regarding employee performance is straightforward. If a staff member asks about a review, I explain that if they are still working for me, they are doing a great job, because if they weren't, they'd already be out the door. I give day-to-day support and feedback on job performance. I don't keep score. I praise and correct in real time, and then we move forward. I believe this makes for a less stressful, more enjoyable workplace.

I don't know if he included my comments in his report, but I hope so. I think it's important for entrepreneurs to retain their independence, because it's what makes us start down the self-employment path in the first place. It's okay to think outside the corporate box. If you have or will start your own company that utilizes a traditional HR department structure, don't be afraid of reigning them in. Their job should be to see that you are compliant with government requirements, not creating their own kingdom.

WHAT MATTERS MOST

Family first. While entrepreneurs are known for working long hours, ensure your greatest passion is for your family.

A FOUNDATION OF TRUST

In my experience, a lasting marriage is among the most rewarding relationships a person can enjoy. I've had the good fortune of sharing my life with my wife Dana for 40-plus years now. I try to show her my commitment to our relationship every day.

When I knew our relationship was getting serious, I asked Dana to give a lot of thought to what her life might be like as a military spouse when I was deployed, possibly for months at a time. She said she didn't need to give it a lot of thought and insisted she'd be fine. She was right. Dana singlehandedly managed our home and cared for our children while I was deployed. We never had any difficulties that we didn't easily overcome. I was grateful for her steadfastness and support during those early years, especially when I watched fellow airmen deal with stress and distraction related to their various marital dramas. Some marriages didn't survive the long work hours and frequent separation. I'm glad ours did.

I'm grateful for her constant support of my business ideas over the years. Even though I do my best to thank her, I think many people who achieve success in business fail to give their spouses the credit they deserve for their role in it.

If you are an entrepreneur, you and your partner both must put in a lot of hours to keep the business and the marriage on course. And you must trust each other.

I vividly remember coming home after abruptly giving my two-week notice to leave my job at Taco Bell Corporate. Doing this turned our world upside down, and I clearly hadn't discussed it with Dana beforehand. It just happened. But did she respond with hysterics? No. No hysterics, no drama. She simply offered her support, and asked what I thought our next move would be. A couple weeks later we learned the next move was a literal one, relocating from Florida to my new job and our new life in Georgia. Dana didn't flinch. She got right to work, packing our belongings and handling the logistics of the move.

If you're wondering how this is possible, I think it's because right from the start we agreed to trust each other to make the right decisions for our family and our future. I'm proud and honored to say our marriage still operates this way all these years later.

CONDITIONS FOR GROWTH

Not long after my son Justin and I were certified to dive we signed up for a trip to West Palm Beach, FL. Since we'd done our certification dives in a lake, we were eager to make our first ocean dives. Sea conditions were okay, but the underwater visibility was terrible. Maybe 10 feet at best. I suggested to Justin we could sit this one out, but he said no. The guide encouraged us, explaining that the visibility might improve once we got past the first 15 feet, so in we went.

We entered the water with three other buddy teams and started our descent, drifting along in a slight current. The visibility did not improve. We really couldn't see much of anything, and to make matters worse, the other divers kept bumping into us. After about 10 minutes of this I signaled for us to end the dive.

This might sound like a terrible experience, but it wasn't. Why? Because I was able to watch Justin calmly manage every aspect of the challenges we experienced. The firsts of diving in the ocean from a boat, the low visibility, the too-close buddies, all of it. On the boat ride back to the dock, I congratulated him on his calmness, saying it was a lot to handle for our first ocean dive together. The other divers overheard us and could not believe it had been our first ocean dive. They admitted they had a logged a lot of dives and they'd struggled more with the conditions than we had.

———

After my daughter Ashley was certified she accompanied me on a trip aboard the *Thailand Aggressor*, on its northern Andaman Islands route. This region occasionally has strong currents, making some dives best suited for experienced divers.

On one dive, the boat was moored in front of an area of large, submerged boulders. The plan was to swim to the mooring line and pull ourselves against a moderate current down the line. Ashley and I waited for the first guests to enter and make their descent before we both entered and started pulling ourselves down the line. When we were about a third of the way down, the first divers were making their way back up, deciding that the current was too strong for their comfort. We all knew not to let go of the line, so they sort of climbed over us. It was a little awkward, but no big deal. Once they passed, we continued our descent until we were a few feet above the boulders. I signaled for Ashley to let go of the line and join the divemaster behind a big row of boulders, dropping out of the current and into a maze of brilliantly colored corals and swirls of fish. The giant rocks created a labyrinth of marine life, which our guide knew like the back of her hand. We had an awesome dive.

After the dive, one of the guests who'd aborted the dive said to me, "That was some current! I can't believe you let your daughter make that dive." She tried to sound congratulatory, but the tone of her voice suggested disapproval. I responded by saying, "She won't know what she's capable of unless she tries. I'll never stop her from trying."

That conversation stayed stuck in my mind. Later, I asked my daughter if she'd had any concerns about the strong current on the way down. She shrugged it off as being part of the adventure. She said it was a fun new way to get to the bottom.

———

In scuba diving, one firm rule is that a diver can "call"—meaning abort or end—a dive, at any time, for any reason or no reason at all. No questions asked. Divers know to respect each other's limits and we don't allow shame or blame backlash when someone calls a dive.

In the stories I just shared about my kids, I will admit I was proud to witness each of them demonstrate a level of physical skill and mental fortitude I hadn't seen before. I was happy to hear them say they enjoyed the challenging dive conditions. But it would have been okay if they had decided to call it. They wouldn't have gotten a lecture from me, because the dives weren't important. What matters most is that our love of diving created opportunities for my then-teenage kids to grow. And we got to enjoy that experience together.

CREATING AND
MANAGING A WORK FAMILY

Throughout this book I've shared that my wife Dana and I are happy having our children and grandchildren close by. Being a part of each other's daily lives is a joy beyond measure.

Recently, I replaced some wood on our back porch railing and was in the process of painting it when one of my young grandsons arrived and asked to help. I grabbed another paintbrush and began teaching him how to paint. He was eager to learn and asked if he could add the paintbrush to his toolbox when we were done. I gave each grandchild their own toolbox when they were about three or four years old. I think it makes sense to teach kids to use a few basic tools, like ones routinely used in household repairs. And it pays to start them out early. I share this story as an example of how you might introduce your family into your business, which is the goal of many entrepreneurs.

I didn't start out with the goal of having my son and daughter, and their spouses, all working with me at Aggressor Adventures. In fact, I thought it might be a bad idea.

Here's why. When my children were still in high school, I read the book *House of Mondavi: The Rise and Fall of an American Wine Dynasty* by Julia Flynn Siler. The book is listed on Amazon as, "An epic, scandal-plagued story of the immigrant family that built—and then spectacularly lost—a global wine empire." When the book was released in 2008 it quickly became a *New York Times'* bestseller, and it remains a compelling read. After I finished it, I emailed the author to tell her how much I enjoyed reading her work. It was clear she'd done exhaustive research on the family and their tumultuous history. To my surprise, she replied to my email, sharing that many West Coast wineries use the book as reference material—a cautionary tale filled with real-life examples of how not to run a family business.

The first mistake Cesare Mondavi made was to put his sons Robert and Peter in competing roles within the company. Perhaps he thought sibling rivalry would push the brothers to each be as successful as possible. If this was the plan, it backfired. The rivalry caused resentment and bitterness that sparked a decades-long blood feud which ultimately destroyed the family empire.

This is a mistake I do not intend to make with my business. Yes, both my children and their spouses work for my company, but I have intentionally avoided the "Mondavi mistake" of putting them in competing roles. I work hard to cultivate a workplace environment in which every employee knows they have an important job to perform, and they are a valuable member of a team. Everyone gets treated the same. We are a "work family" that includes my actual family members among my valued employees.

I've long-since let go of my early concerns about hiring my family. I enjoy getting to interact with them daily and I'm thrilled to see them thriving in their respective roles within the company. Perhaps the future might one day include welcoming the next generation, our grandkids, into the business.

NOTES ON MANTA RAYS AND MANKIND

As divers, we are infatuated with the vastness and variety of the underwater world. Some divers are after the big stuff, the sharks and whales and manta rays. Others delight in finding tiny nudibranchs not much bigger than a grain of rice. Still others love the history of shipwrecks or the challenges of technical diving or underwater photography. There is literally something for divers of all interests and skill levels.

Diving provides us with the incentive to travel to the far ends of the earth, but our travels also enrich our lives with the opportunity to experience and learn about different cultures.

The Sultanate of Oman is a country in southwestern Asia, on the Arabian Peninsula. I recently visited Oman to enjoy diving off the Arabian Sea, then spent several days touring the countryside. The friendliness of the Omani people was evident everywhere I went. I visited many historical sites, including the Grand Mosque in Muscat, which is the largest and most magnificent mosque in the country. The complex is massive, covering nearly five million square feet. The main chandelier above the praying hall is nearly 50 feet tall and encompasses a spiral staircase attendants use when changing the chandelier's more than 1,000 light bulbs.

Despite the mosque's extraordinary beauty, my most memorable experience wasn't the architecture or the grandeur of its interior. It was the people. At the end of the tour, visitors are invited to meet the prayer leaders, known as imams. My guide insisted they'd be welcoming and to my delight, they were very friendly. They didn't preach or try to force their doctrine on me. They were there for my questions, period. And their answers were thoughtful and genuine. We enjoyed a mutually rewarding cultural exchange, which included their asking me about my life and family in the USA. It was an amazing, enriching discussion, one I will treasure forever.

Mark Twain hit the nail on the head when he said, "Travel is fatal to prejudice, bigotry and narrow-mindedness." I've witnessed these deaths when interacting with people out walking the streets of Sorong, Indonesia, in the remote mountains of Thailand, and while cruising the Nile River in Egypt. I'm routinely approached with kindness and curiosity by people who want to share with me and learn about me.

Social media has helped me stay in contact with friends from all over the world. My Facebook/Meta contacts are comprised of multinational guests I have meet on our adventures, local staff and crew members, tour guides and random people I meet while traveling. I am always pleased when they wish me a Happy Fourth of July or Merry Christmas and I return the sentiment when they are celebrating their religious and national holidays. I'm grateful that this is one of the ways the Internet can bring people closer together.

IN PRAISE OF SLOWNESS

'll admit, I'm always on the go. I'm happy that my life is fast paced, but you'll never see me get in a hurry when I'm on a scuba dive. Experience has taught me that if I rush around underwater, I might cover a lot of distance, but I'll miss out on what's happening around me.

I think that as divers, we tend to get over-excited and want to see everything all at once. Moving slowly and going with the flow, or just hovering motionless above a small patch of reef is how you're likely get the most out of a scuba dive. When you look closely at the reef, you'll see fascinating behaviors unfolding, including cleaning, courtship, and predation, just to name a few.

When diving in the South Pacific, I noticed a unicornfish move into a cleaning station. It positions its body head down and changes color, turning almost white to signal its desire to be cleaned. On cue, a cleaner wrasse and several tiny shrimps began quickly picking parasites off the unicornfish. This behavior is called mutualism because the cleaners get a meal, and the fish gets rid of unwanted hitchhikers. Divers can observe this behavior at cleaning stations on reefs all over the world, but only if we move slowly enough that we don't spook the fish.

In Belize, I once watched in awe as a pair of indigo hamlets carried out a long and intricate courtship dance before finally spawning. Not far from the hamlets, I saw a pair of sergeant majors engaging in the same mating ritual. While all this flirty stuff was happening, I noticed a barracuda on the same patch of reef, scanning the area for a potential meal.

Among my favorite underwater relationships to witness is the odd pairing of the goby and the blind shrimp. They live together on the seafloor, in a hole which the shrimp is constantly bulldozing. Since the shrimp is blind, the goby stands guard at the entrance to their burrow. If it senses danger, the goby taps the shrimp with its tail and together they disappear down the hole. To view this fascinating relationship divers must remain as still and as patient as possible. Startle the pair and you'll be left staring at a hole in the sand.

A few years ago, I spent nearly an entire scuba dive on a not-so-special section of reef under the *Turks & Caicos Aggressor* while other divers headed to the main attraction, a spectacular wall where we routinely see Caribbean reef sharks. I hovered over a corkscrew anemone for a long while, noticing several tiny, translucent Pederson shrimps bouncing in and out of its tentacles. This is a common sight, but then I noticed they weren't the only creatures living amongst the anemone's tentacles. What at first glance appeared to be a small dark spec turned out to be the tiniest juvenile conch I've ever seen! It turns out that little patch of reef was special after all.

IF IT'S WORTH IT, STICK WITH IT

In the summer of 2023, Dana and I spent a week on the *BVI Aggressor* with my family and a few friends. Both of my children, their spouses and all four grandchildren joined us. My oldest grandchild, Bennett, turned 10 the previous November. He was excited to turn "double digits" because at age 10 a minor can become certified as a Junior Open Water Diver.

All the grandkids are little water bugs. I introduced them to scuba in our backyard pool when each was three years old, letting them float at the surface, breathing from a scuba regulator. At age six, a kid can enroll in Scuba Rangers, a program designed to introduce them to scuba gear and how it works. It teaches the basic theories kids need to understand to safely scuba dive in a swimming pool under the direct supervision of an instructor.

Since I'm an active Instructor Trainer, I had the pleasure of certifying Bennett as a Scuba Ranger and took him through the Junior Open Water course, too. We completed his academic and swimming pool sessions before the BVI trip. Now, we'd finish his training in the ocean during our family vacation.

This part of the course involves the student demonstrating mastery of all the skills outlined by the certification agency during a series of dives while under the supervision of an instructor. I'm proud to say that Bennett did a great job on his first two dives, but later in the day he confided that he had concerns about a skill he'd be required to demonstrate the following day. Mask removal/replacement had him spooked. The skill of mask removal/replacement is exactly that; the diver removes their mask underwater, replaces it, and clears it of water. The skill isn't technically difficult to perform, but some scuba students find it challenging.

Although Bennett had performed the mask removal skill perfectly during our swimming pool sessions, he was afraid he might not be able to do it in the ocean. He asked if he could do a practice session in the ocean, just to be certain. I could have said, "You know this skill. The fear is all in your head. You don't need more practice. You just need to quit worrying." But instead of dismissing his fears and refusing his request for the extra practice, I agreed. It turns out, he did have a mental block about the skill. He had performed it easily in the swimming pool, but he was struggling with it in the ocean. Still, he stuck with it and kept trying. Before long he was removing and replacing the mask, no problem. The next day on the training dive, he aced it.

———

When a new Open Water Diver completes their certification on an Aggressor Liveaboard, we "make them a cake" to celebrate their achievement. Bennett knew about this tradition and was excited that I'd be the one overseeing the ceremony, which takes place on the yacht's swim platform. Bennett beamed as I dumped a bowl of cake flour on his head, then cracked a few raw eggs on top, covered his head in chocolate syrup and finished the recipe with a big squirt of whipped cream. I "made him a cake" as the rest of our family watched from the dive deck, cheering. Bennett was a smiling, sticky mess. And I was one proud Papa.

———

It matters that Bennett completed his goal of getting certified. But what matters most is that at the tender age of 10, he was self-possessed enough to admit he was fearful and ask for help to work through his fears. I know a lot of grown-ups who lack this kind of confidence and might give up instead of asking for help. And unfortunately, I know a few who, instead of helping, would tease a person for admitting their fear.

THE RED SOLO CUP OF ENRICHMENT

I listen to a lot of podcasts and read a lot of books on a wide range of topics. A while back I was listening to a podcast featuring Kyle Petty, who was promoting his bestselling book, *Swerve or Die: Life at My Speed in the First Family of NASCAR Racing*. If you're not a race fan, you might not know that Kyle Petty is considered NASCAR royalty. He's the grandson of racing champion Lee Petty and the only son of NASCAR's winningest driver ever, Richard Petty.

Kyle won his first-ever stock-car race, the Daytona ARCA 200, in 1979 at age 18. Already living in the family spotlight, this win earned Kyle his own celebrity status. Despite this, Petty wasn't content to just follow in the family business. He blazed his own trail, which in addition to the race world included careers in country music, working in the film industry, and philanthropic endeavors. These days, he's often seen covering pre- and post-NASCAR events for various news outlets.

During the podcast, Petty explained that the book about his life isn't just a bunch of "glory days" stories. Yes, there are some, because he's had quite a few glory days. But he also includes his personal and professional triumphs and tragedies and shares that his overarching goal is to just to be a good person. Apparently, his readers agree. One of the reviews of Petty's book posted on Amazon says, "For a guy that could be a prick because of who he is, he is just the greatest, most down-to-earth person."

Petty's interview got me thinking about the title of this book, and why I'm attempting to explain what enrichment means to me, and how I define success.

My business success has allowed me the opportunity to meet influential people, including presidents and ambassadors gathered in luxuriously appointed dining rooms full of diamond-studded multi-billionaires. I've attended events during which I've raised a ridiculously expensive Champagne glass filled with ridiculously expensive Champagne, to toast the health of the very wealthy people whose sole purpose for attending the event was to increase their wealth or advance their status. We shared polite conversation, and we enjoyed a delicious five-course gourmet meal. And in most instances, when the meal was done, I've left feeling hungry. But for what?

For connection.

It's not that they're not nice people, because they are very nice. Most of them are geniuses who've developed hugely successful businesses and they do a lot of worthy philanthropic work, too. But I've just never felt like I'm on the same wavelength with that crowd in terms of what enrichment means. To me, they seem to always be seeking fulfillment because there's never enough. They appear to always be wanting more.

Perhaps it's my small-town southern roots running deep, but I'll take a simple backyard barbecue with real friends and a Red Solo cup filled with a local brew over the status-climbing celebrity event, any day. I want to truly enjoy the company of the people I choose to have in my life. I think this is why I like spending so much time with my family, my work team, and the divers who go on our adventures.

WHAT RETIREMENT?

Dana and I recently attended a Frankie Valli concert. Frankie is 85 years old now, and he's the sole remaining original member of the Four Seasons. At age 85 he's still putting on a great show and his fans love him. In fact, a couple people seated in front of us had traveled from south Florida to Augusta, GA to see him. They said they attend several of his concerts a year. This made me curious about his tour, so I went online and discovered that his 2024 touring schedule includes nearly 60 appearances. I also noticed he's got bookings scheduled through 2026.

I thought, why not? He's been touring since 1953 so he must love doing it. Why stop?

I've reached the age when some people consider early retirement. Recently, several friends have retired, and they're always asked, "When are you retiring?" I can't say I haven't thought about it. Maybe one day there's a switch that flips and I decide I want to go do something else. But that hasn't happened yet, and I don't imagine it will anytime soon.

When asked about retirement, a lot of people say they retired because they wanted to spend more time with their family. But Dana and I spend time together every day and we travel together quite often. And since both our son and daughter and their spouses all work at Aggressor Adventures, going to work each day means I get to spend time with them, so the "so I can spend more time with family" reason for retirement won't hold up for me! We see our grandkids practically every day, too. They live close enough that the older ones can ride their bikes.

I love everything about running my business. I love opening new destinations and being out on adventures with our guests. I love meeting whatever challenges arise. Even though I can't carry a tune in a bucket, and I don't think of myself as an entertainer, I think I have a lot in common with

Frankie Valli. We both are doing what we love to do, which is entertaining people and making them happy. Never mind retirement. I think I'll be like Frankie and just keep doing what I love.

SEA OF CHANGE

'm a big local sports fan. When I was in the Taco Bell franchise business, I was always happy to sponsor youth sports, especially little league teams. I also sponsored local police trading cards, charitable fundraisers, parades and events that involved community engagement.

Some business owners get annoyed by requests for donations, or what they perceive as people "begging" for money. I see it differently. The community operates like an ecosystem. Each community member relies on other members to grow and thrive. Proximity helps create personal relationships. Sponsoring a team or in some other way supporting community engagement helps a business position itself close to people. These people are neighbors, not "beggars." Allocating some of my budget to fund youth sports was a good investment in kids' growth and the growth of my franchises. If a team of happy, hungry little leaguers visited one of my Taco Bells after a game, it was a win-win. Even if they opted to have a post-game picnic in a park instead of eating at Taco Bell, it was still money well invested in the community.

When I purchased Aggressor Fleet in 2007, I wanted to continue the practice of charitable giving, this time with added focus on the marine environment. I started researching marine-oriented charities and began learning about programs the fleet's destinations were currently involved in. It turned out that while many of the destinations had robust community engagement and charitable giving programs, several destinations didn't have much involvement other than the occasional donation to a local fundraiser. I wanted to find a way to weave community service and charitable giving into the cultural fabric of the company. I set out to identify an existing marine conservation organization that our scuba diving customers loved, figuring we'd align with them.

My practice is to always learn about a charity's financials before I commit funds. It's shocking to discover that some charitable organizations spend the bulk of donors' money paying administrative costs like salaries and office space, with little left over to fund their programs. Their intentions might be good, but at the end of the day, not much progress gets made. After reviewing all the marine-related charities that I thought fit within the guidelines I want to associate Aggressor Fleet with, I didn't find a good match.

Always knowing there is a solution to every problem, I opted to start my own 501(c)3 charitable organization. I challenged myself to guarantee that 100 percent of all donated funds goes straight to our conservation and education initiatives. No overhead, no administrative expenses. To make it work, Aggressor Fleet would cover the salary of a newly created staffer, the Director of Conservation and Outreach, who would oversee the fleet's internal sustainability program while also serving as the Director of the newly formed Sea of Change Foundation, at no cost to the nonprofit. We chose the name Sea of Change because it was a sea change in how a charity would direct its funds.

I networked within the dive community to fill Aggressor's new position of Conservation and Outreach. I have always felt a personal recommendation is worth more than a beefy resume'. I was fortunate to find and hire a person who fit the dual job description perfectly.

We immediately created and implemented a new Green the Fleet initiative, aimed at finding economical ways of upping our energy efficiency, reducing single-use plastics, using sustainably sourced products, and doing more recycling. This program continues to celebrate a lot of little Green the Fleet wins that our guests appreciate, and we're extending this important work fleet-wide.

When it came time to select a board of directors, we invited several leading scuba industry members, all of whom were stunned to learn that 100 percent of our funds would serve conservation efforts, with zero overhead. We didn't ask them for "seed money" donations as is the norm, but rather got right to work discussing potential fund-raising projects. Within the first few minutes of our initial board meeting, I knew I'd picked an amazing team to serve on our board. With their support, we were able to quickly fund Sea of Change and begin accepting applications from potential grant applicants.

One of my most consistently active board members and a true leader in the scuba diving industry, Doug McNeese, had an established charity that awarded grants to scuba diving leaders from around the world. We met to discuss a collaboration between his organization and Sea of Change, thinking we could do even greater good by teaming up. This joint fund-raising auction sponsored by both our organizations has become our biggest annual income source. And still, 100 percent of Sea of Change donations support grants and scholarships.

What matters most is that if you and your company are making charitable contributions, it pays to do a bit of investigative work before you hand over your hard-earned cash. Make sure the nonprofit does a good job of managing their funds and following through on their promises. As a rule of thumb, smaller, well-run charities with low overhead tend to serve their mission more fully than global powerhouses that often waste millions on salaries and lavish fund-raising parties.

DEFINING SUCCESS

I was very lucky to find out early in my career that delivering customer service at the highest levels is how I define business success. It is what drives me every day. And it's what helped form the foundation for my personal success in life, too.

Don't get caught up worrying about how others define success, or what they do to achieve it. What matters is that you come up with your own definition of success, and then live up to it. If you work hard for it, you can achieve it.

So how do you achieve success?

Be realistic. Not every kid that starts out wanting to be an astronaut or a fighter pilot walks on the moon or earns Top Gun status. I'm not suggesting you don't pursue your dreams. Absolutely go after your dreams, the bigger the better, but set realistic goals. Aim for success one step at a time and work your way to the top. You know the old saying, "slow and steady wins the race."

Next, face facts. Make all your decisions based on facts, not emotions. I've heard so much about "trust your gut and just go for it" but that's not great advice, at least not in my opinion. I suggest you research your goals, know what it will take to succeed and map out a fact-driven plan to achieve them. If you rely on what you "feel like" doing you might end up going around in circles, working hard but going nowhere.

Keep going. Once you have a few small wins, keep at it. Keep reinvesting in yourself, by staying curious and learning new things. Do this and the world will continue to open up to you.

And remember, true, lasting success is not rags to riches; it is rags to enrichment.

RECOMMENDED READING

Dove
By Robin L. Graham

On Bullshit
By Harry G. Frankfurt

Known and Unknown:
A Memoir
By Donald Rumsfeld

Swerve or Die:
Life at My Speed in the First Family of NASCAR Racing
By Kyle Petty

The House of Mondavi:
The Rise and Fall of an American Wine Dynasty
By Julia Flynn Siler

BONUS CONTENT

Scan the QR code for bonus content, including photos, videos and interviews.

ACKNOWLEDGMENTS

Writing this book has been an adventure. I want to acknowledge the following people for helping *From Rags to Enrichment* come to life:

To my family, thank you for encouraging me to write this book and for allowing me to include stories that describe how we blend our personal lives, professional lives, and passions in ways that serve us well. Above all, if you are happy, my life is enriched.

To my work family at Aggressor Adventures, thank you for making sure the business never missed a beat while I was setting aside time for writing. I appreciate your dedication.

To my editor/publisher, Cathryn Castle Garcia, thank you for asking questions that helped me dig deeper during the writing process. Without your guidance this would have been a very short, very boring book!

www.ingramcontent.com/pod-product-compliance
Lightning Source LLC
Chambersburg PA
CBHW060835110426
R18122100001BA/R181221PG42736CBX00036BA/45